Ang[...]
the Keys to
Paradise

Ancient Egyptian Codes
to Open Your Door to Heaven

FINDHORN PRESS

Angels and the Keys to Paradise

Ancient Egyptian Codes
to Open Your Door to Heaven

Stewart Pearce

FINDHORN PRESS

Copyright © 2014 by Stewart Pearce

The right of Stewart Pearce to be identified as the author
of this work has been asserted by him in accordance with the
Copyright, Designs and Patents Act 1998.

Published in 2014 by Findhorn Press, Scotland

ISBN 978-1-84409-631-2

A CIP record for this title is available from the British Library.

Edited by Michael Hawkins
Front cover design and illustrations by Richard Crookes
Interior by Thierry Bogliolo
Printed and bound in the European Union

Published by
Findhorn Press
117-121 High Street,
Forres IV36 1AB,
Scotland, UK

t +44 (0)1309 690582
f +44 (0)131 777 2711
e info@findhornpress.com
www.findhornpress.com

Contents

PROLOGUE: Prophecy   7

1   The KHAT   21
2   The REN   41
3   The SHEW   61
4   The SEKHEM   77
5   The KA   91
6   The AB   109
7   The BA   127
8   The SAHU   149
9   The AKHU   161
10   The Keys to Paradise   179

EPILOGUE: Ascension   199

PROPHECY

*If, each day, we pledge to make our lives better than when we first
began them; if, each hour, we fully open our hearts in kindness to one
another; if, each minute, we truly can unfold our arms to the miracle
of creation, making life more beautiful than when we first found it;
if, each second, we give an act of love, intended to inspire someone else
to do the same – we give a gift to immortality. Each time we give an
act of love, the energy field of our heart beacons a light so bright that a
Temple of Paradise is created and the gates therein spring wide.*

– THE HEART'S NOTE, STEWART PEARCE

Archangel Jophiel is the key-keeper to the Gates of Paradise, and as such,
this Divine Liberator originally arose from the Atlantean ether, entering
our midst as a beautiful Yellow Orb. Then, once the end times of Atlantis
had occurred, Jophiel informed the sacred priesthood and Pharaohic coun-
sels of Egypt.

Jophiel means the 'beauty of God' and, as such, this extraordinary Angel champions the essence of liberation and detachment, whilst also advo-
cating the vow of forgiveness, pledging that all sentient beings subscribe to
its felicity. It is with these passions that Jophiel resides over the great gates
of Osiris Paradise.

Jophiel is as hallowed as Creation itself, liberated by the life of the Cosmos to be an Angel of transformation – a force that operates through a ray
of plasma as bright as any Citrine could possibly be – for Jophiel's unique
signature on Earth is written in the power of that beautiful mineral. Therefore, contemplating Citrine means that detachment and liberation are
stimulated within us by Jophiel's decree, as the mineral gives its soul to the
possibility of freedom's joy. Try gazing into the precious light of Jophiel's
icon, feel the whisper of freedom arising from the Orb, for this is the core
message of this Angel's teaching.

ANGELIC LEGENDS OF OLD

There exists an ancient legend of how Jophiel brought the 'detachment' of the yellow ray to Earth, to pass through the mineral of Citrine. This took place during the liberation of Adam and Eve from their protected innocence within the Garden of Eden.

When the Divine knowledge of innocence and grace had been experienced through the vibration of Adam and Eve and all living entities, the energy within 'time' brought forth the degree that the vibration of the garden must transform, must ascend to a higher octave. Therefore, Archangel Jophiel of the Malachim Angels gave us Citrine as a 'calling stone' to bring about liberation and freedom in the purest way possible. The Malachim were the Archangels who carried out God's original purpose.

So please view the icon of Jophiel's beautiful Citrine Orb that begins this prologue, and you will see an exquisite Sigil within the Orb of Jophiel – the Sigils are magical symbols containing the essence of a revered substance, and here are seen as eternal geometries containing the heart of each Archangel. They draw into them celestial forces of great magnitude. Therefore, reviewing the Sigil's beauty means we experience the very essence of freedom itself and, just like the wistful beauty of Macchu Picchu , which has always conveyed the wonder of spiritual freedom, contemplating this image will uplift you and allow you to experience the anticipation of spiritual freedom and adventure in its most lucid form. Please gaze on the Sigil, and you will feel Jophiel's heart becoming at one with yours, urging you towards the liberation of your spirit.

Liberation can be risky and bold, involving uncertain outcomes. Yet, within the experience of adventure, our souls take flight and expand as we face any specific challenge. Our souls perpetuity moves us through the fear, encouraging us to develop through the unexpected possibilities that are conjured forth, and so we shine through victory over the fear. Thus we resolve karmic lesions; thus we rise to a higher vibration of thought and feeling; thus we radiate wise, loving, glorious dimensions of being; thus we experience a sense of jubilance, and the most precious jewel of the Cosmos shines through us – **Love**.

THE GATES AND KEYS OF PARADISE

The Gates and Keys to Paradise in this form were first shown to me during a profound shift in consciousness during the Winter Solstice of 2012. I'd chosen to be in Egypt for the remarkable cosmic rite of passage known as 12.12.12, and with a group of souls who had also journeyed with me through the work of the Temple of Sound Healing known as the Alchemy of Voice.

This unique Temple reflects the work of the Angels of Atlantis who requested that I create a spiritual pathway dedicated to their unique collective re-emergence, when they appeared to me in 1987. The Temple arises from the intelligence and compassion of the heart, and as sound is at the core of creation, the temple work is designed to tune the personality of voice with the sacred breath-prana of the soul.

The essential work is formed by twelve pillars or workshops, which permit all who attend to tune their body's unique signature note, the song of our soul, bringing it into alignment with their life purpose. This occurs firstly by integrating the physical, emotional, mental and spiritual bodies by healing any lesion, and then by feeling an expression of this harmony along the sacred path of life.

The work means we have context to surrender our lives into the hands of spirit, creating Heaven on Earth, whilst soaring into the heart of God, into the very centre of the Garden of Paradise. Thus we connect with the code of the great I AM PRESENCE – the true identity that is the unique individualization of Almighty God within each person.

THE RESURRECTION RETREAT

This Retreat was a specific part of the Temple work, as our unfolding passions led us to December 2012 and, specifically, we decided this experience of Egypt would become a time for Resurrection. So we consciously designed the journey to be an opportunity to literally die to our old selves, and then to create them anew, as resurrected lives, yet void of karma.

We had chosen this as a consequence of the Winter Solstice, when we knew that the time of minimum light in the northern hemisphere, marked one of the most auspicious days in the life of the Universe for over 26,000 years – a time when the planets of our Solar System would be in alignment with the Galactic Heart.

Twenty-eight of us had decided to travel to the Throat Chakra of the world – to the ancient city of Luxor – to recalibrate and reform ourselves, to resurrect the purity of our souls, and to take on the form of our light bodies. We felt the desire to become beings of the new millennia, evolving as Homo luminous, or at least as close as we could muster, living in Divine light.

We all saw this as a great opportunity for expiating our karma, and therefore of becoming wiser, more mature, or certainly better people than before. We believed this to be a noble way of serving the evolution of our planet and everything that exists upon her. Our pledge was simple: that we would surrender to divine love, allowing the sacred to shine through our lives with a force of truth and transparency, so that we could literally become beacons of unconditional love.

During the Retreat, we planned to visit many of the astro-geographical Temples along the beautiful River Nile, which would prove to be a very specific pathway of ritual exploration. Remarkably, each Temple was designed, both in its Earthly presence, and within its Heavenly vibration, to bring about an aspect of profound healing within the physical experience of human life – our lives – and that of the Universe.

THE KEYS IN THE TEMPLE OF OSIRIS

During one such visit – to the fabled Temple of Karnak (the Temple of Constant Creation), which holds within its walls the mysteries of ancient Egypt's spiritual philosophy – my guide Ashraf Amin asked me if I wished to experience a hitherto unknown Chapel attributed to Osiris. Osiris was the King God for the ancient Egyptians, whose Chapel was positioned on the east side of this vast Temple complex.

Earlier in visits to ancient Egypt I had become completely entranced by the notion of this Chapel, for its walls held evidence of the Gates and Keys to Paradise, and marked a portal-connection between our mortal flesh and the immortal soul. So I was particularly excited about visiting it, and felt Archangel Jophiel's presence urging me forward.

Being there was absolutely wonderful for the Chapel's crystal energy was palpable and, in one section of the Temple's sacred architecture, the divine Ankh keys were clearly illustrated. The keys were used by the High Priests to lead the Pharaoh Initiates through a process called Osirification – a rite of passage by which the soul of the Pharaoh could become emblazoned within human form. The KHAT body of the Pharaoh was destined to become a cosmic listening post in an ocean of sound, the aspiration of the noble lineage.

Osirification was a similar practice to the Asian spiritual rite known as the Kundalini Awakening, which is mostly experienced within devotion of Hindu and Buddhist practice. Kundalini occurs when a force charged by God, called Shaktipat, is given directly from a Spiritual Teacher such as a Swami to the initiate. Kundalini occurs after the preparation and concentration of a disciplined meditation practice, and is mostly seen as a coiled Serpent awakening in the base of the spine, then spreading throughout the whole body of the individual, enlightening cells with fire-filled Pranayama.

In ancient Egypt, the Pharaohs, and possibly a few of the High Priests, known as God's emissaries on Earth, could experience Osirification. The Pharaohs were destined to evolve towards Ascension, to travel through the varying octaves of Earth force into Paradise, and thence to Nirvana. In ancient Egypt, this refined state of being was known as the AKHU condition – a state of absolute bliss and one-ness with the Divine.

Experiencing the Chapel was simply phenomenal for there, carved on the walls, were the seven Ankhs, the keys that open the varying vistas of consciousness through which we are led to enlightenment. This Egyptian tradition of enlightenment means the highly evolved initiate may pass into paradise whilst in flesh, rather than leaving the body merely at the point of our death.

Also, carved on the Temple walls, were the seven Gates of Paradise. Except it appeared that the Priests, who were adept practitioners in the art of Telekinesis and Teleportation, had literally moved the geometry of the walls around, to confound those who viewed the temple. This must have been an ubiquitous act in the ancient world, so as to confuse the un-initiated traveller from fully seeing the mysteries which held such psychic power. Consequently, the secret spells and ritual acts were hidden, saving them from being adulterated or misused by those of corrupt intention. The Priests fervently believed that if the power of the sacred tools were placed into the wrong hands, chaos would ensue.

On the walls of the Temple of Denderah it is written:

> *Everything sacred is blessed, everything blessed is sacred – only those who tread the path of righteous thought shall enter the Temple for elevation to the company of the Neters (Gods and Goddesses)*

Yet there was more to be shared, for whilst viewing these sacred tools, Archangel Jophiel appeared and instructed me to visit the Valley of the Kings, as there a rare Tomb would be opened for us to investigate. This came as divine providence so that we could feel first hand the remarkable secrets of the ancient world, of how the unique astrological portal of December 21st, 2012 would impinge on our lives, and herald a window of Divine revelation for our own accelerated consciousness. I was told that specific energies were to be released, enabling another level of planetary incarnation to succeed. However, I didn't experience the full impact of this remarkable Tomb and its Treasures until April 2013.

Jophiel as the Divine Liberator directed me to visit the Valley of the Baboons, to ultimately meet Thoth, my Master, who amusingly used the garrulous Baboon as a means to manifest spirit teaching on the planet. The ancient Egyptians believed all Baboons to be vessels that were inhabited by the Gods, and so the Baboon held several lofty positions in Egyptian mythology, largely as a creature of the underworld, and therefore of the Dead.

The Baboon God, BABA, gave rise to the animals name, and as Baboons greet the dawning Sun with screeching sounds, outstretched waving arms, and a jumping happy disposition, they were also considered animals of Creation, and thus respected for their close association with the Sun God RE.

Hitherto, Baboons became closely associated with the great Thoth, the God of Alchemy, Wisdom, Science and the Sacred Word, and as Thoth's sacred animal, the baboon was often depicted on Tombs and Temple walls directing the Scribes in their many tasks. Thoth was also a part representation of the God of the Moon, and so Baboons were often shown wearing the crescent moon on their heads whilst they carried out Thoth's duties. Similarly, Baboons were often portrayed in ancient hieroglyphics holding the scales that weighed the heart of the deceased, for example in the ceremony of the judgment of the dead, for Baboons were seen to guard the first gate of the underworld in the *Egyptian Book of the Dead*.

The Valley of the Baboons, alone and somewhat forlorn, holds one of the most sacred Tombs of Ancient Egypt, that of the High Priest AY, who gave his life in service to RA, Pharaoh Akhenaten and his significant son Tutankhamun. Father and Son were extraordinary beings and noted through the annals of history as two of the most significant Pharaohs in the evolution of ancient Egypt's Priesthood. The Priests virtually governed the complex process of the country's politics and exchequer, which functioned as a sacred economy.

The Priests held beliefs that tethered the hierarchy of their kingdom to the Divine mysteries, believing that all abundance arose from the benefaction of the sixty-four Gods and Goddesses, the well-being of the Pharaoh, the life of the Sacred Nile, and the people's loving vitality. Positioned thus meant to be in constant veneration of their Gods and Goddesses, and so all aspects of life were considered sacred.

As we moved along the valley approaching the Tomb of AY, the Guards suggested our access to the Tomb of AY would be prohibited, as a consequence of a mysterious electrical failure – literally the lights had suddenly malfunctioned.

These crusty old men always appear to me as though they've been in attendance at the Tombs and Temples of Egypt for thousands of years, and yet at the same time aren't particularly interested or cognizant of the vast spiritual and psychic energies emanating from these fabled monuments.

Instead, the Valley held many unseen Guardians, standing in spiritual fervor, observing us intensely, as we passed along the long drive to the Tomb. These beings – Ghostly Priests assigned from another time to protect the secrets – indicated that entry to the sacred Tomb would only be afforded to the devoted initiate. I fully acknowledged them, and psychically asked the 'watchers' for permission. Permission came, yet Grace would only be granted if we entered with pure hearts and minds, and so we determined to be fully reverent of the sacred ways, and thus we prepared to enter with the ancient Priests complementing our ardour.

THE VOICE OF THE HIGH PRIEST AY

The Tomb itself was accessed by a descent of about fifty metres (fifty yards), a gaping gash deep into the bowels of the Earth but, because no electricity lit the stairwell, a definite challenge was raised. Feeling undeterred, I asked Thoth and Jophiel for protection, requesting that my retreat friends move very carefully and with great stealth down into the sacred Tomb. We vowed in our hearts that if we sensed any potential danger, we could guard against anyone receiving a psychic emission, slipping or falling. We needed to be absolutely present, and sheer-footed in mind and body. Then we could gain easy access to the heart of the place, which in turn would assist our soul's journey through death and life. We said our silent but palpable prayers for ease of passage.

Suddenly, as though from nowhere, a Guard stepped forward whose presence hadn't been registered before – a young man named Achmed with piercing light brown eyes, and who gladly suggested he would accompany us. As we descended into the ancient Tomb, he produced a small yet highly effective candle from his Galabia pocket – a touching oddity I thought, as I produced a lighter to give life to the wax – a candle that perhaps came from some distant period of antiquity?

There we were, pouring into the funeral chamber of AY, almost sliding over the rather steep wooden staircase that led into the very womb of the Valley of the Baboons, and the vaulted death chamber constructed 3,300 years before. The Tomb was constructed in veneration of the great High Priest and so, with feelings of great awe and trepidation, we slowly trod each step, breathing each breath with solemn prayers and a sense of immense awe and privilege – yet also in anticipation of something highly unusual about to brim into our lives.

When we had achieved access to the chamber, we stood in keen silence, feeling ourselves once more stable on the even rock, thank heavens, whilst we searched with our purblind eyes into the purple darkness, attempting to see the rich frescoes on the walls – hieroglyphs of uncommon import – an entire wall of surprisingly reverential Baboons, Ay's wife full of blessings and lamentations, the High Priest's veneration to the great Osiris, and a vast granite sarcophagus draped in Isis's flying wings, with the ubiquitous Scarab – symbols of the everlasting life to come!

The silence was deafening, and one or two of us fought for breath to balance our bodies in relation to the immense energy of the place. Gently, I began the Sacred Sonic Meditation Ritual, measured specifically for this unique experience, through which we hoped to gain direct teaching from AY about Akhenaten and Tutankhamun. Surprisingly, our Islamic guide joined in with our chant, producing his own prayerful lamentation, yet synchronizing with our OM. We felt honored that he could create his own prayerful chant, as the sound moved like glimmering incandescence throughout the Tomb Chamber.

I could feel the energy of the unseen Priests who had built the chamber, perhaps for someone as august as Akhenaten himself, chanting their solemn chants and prayers, lighting up the space by their spells, and warming our own offerings with their immense intelligence and grace. Seemingly the musty smell of the place became filled with sweet incense, illuminated by small flickering lights, which brought a rare magic to the ether, alongside the distant chanting of reverberant choruses, which would cease as soon as we paused. We were being steeped in an otherworldly process of profound intention!

The acoustic was simply awe-inspiring, and many of the group became deeply moved by the weighty resonant power of our chanting which, cadence by cadence, floated throughout the sacred space, urging us to gain even greater momentum, to give our 'all' to the memory of AY, and in praise of his immense contribution to Akhenaten's ministry. In reaching a sonic height in our prayerful song our Guide suddenly screamed, dropped the only light we possessed, outside of our own souls, onto the floor, which meant our candlelight was immediately gutted.

There we were, utterly knocked out of our skin by the dramatic transformation of the Guide, with me groping the floor of the Tomb in search of the errant candle, attempting to calm my compatriots, some of whom had moved from our original sacred reverie into sounds of fretful concern, in fear of the darkness, its supernatural power, and what appeared to be the somewhat erratic behavior of our Guide.

I found the candle, and suddenly Achmed became silent. The stillness was deafening after the volume of the sound emitted, and once again I lit the candle as the only way to see balance – thank God for my lighter!

I turned the light on Achmed who had become deadly still, with eyes closed and arms perfunctorily extended in full death position, just like a Mummy.

Then as I moved forward in the stillness, and Achmed suddenly opened his eyes, yet was no longer Achmed, no longer was he the smiling young man I had met forty-five minutes before. Instead what greeted me were the eyes of a much older man – Achmed's face had transmogrified into a completely different being, and in this state he moved forward to bless me with outstretched hands, like the many figures seen in the Temple frescoes, offering grace or gifts to Osiris and RE or RA. This done, he placed a hand on my head, then my heart and, as he touched me, an ancient elixir seemed to seep into my skin and through my veins – Achmed had become the High Priest AY!

I received his grace in full respect, and then steered him throughout the group, whilst he similarly blessed each person, asking us to fully open our hearts to his ancient offering and sacredness.

All this was immensely moving, and we felt an intense yet intimate energy seeping through our consciousness, and so we quaked with the ancient mysterious force of AY moving through each cell of our bodies, changing us forever, reminding us of the deep ecstasy secreted in all of us, that we are spiritual beings on a human journey dispensing love and excellence throughout our creative expressions.

I heard the words of AY reverberating through my soul, whilst closing the door of the ritual through further chanting and a final prayer, whilst AY once more became Achmed. What I heard was:

Give your life to create the new as a gift of spirit, and you will endure the passing of time in full tranquility., for life is not happening to you, life is responding to you! Therefore, live the experience of your thoughts and feelings whilst fermenting your intuition, which is 'seeing with your soul', and I will give you further mysteries to change your life, and the lives of those who venture into this magic with you. ALL IS WELL for Thoth is with you as your Guide.

I trembled as I heard these words, and as we slowly climbed the fifty meters to the light and air of the floating desert above, the Valley of the Baboons. For we each knew that a deep and unalterable place within our beings had been changed forever, altered by the intoxicating aroma of AY's LOVE. This filled each of us with an ineluctable serenity, and we all pledged that we would hold this for as long as we could muster.

Silently, we moved upwards through the darkness, needing no light to guide us, for an inner light led the way. And, as words became redundant, we processed the immense truths that had stirred in our beings from AY's delectable 3,300 year-old pronouncements – the spells we had received in our hearts, which the entire co-creative experience had brought to us.

Post experience, we all needed to touch normality by returning to our hotel and, after eating a nutritious lunch, we folded into a siesta, and much greater internal processing.

THE TEACHINGS OF AY

AY remained in my consciousness for some time and, in conversation with my Egyptologist Guide Ash, I discovered he knew a Holy Man or Magi in Luxor with whom I could perhaps process the information AY had given me. Ashraf said he would explore the idea, and then later called me to suggest that he had found the right person for me to meet, and that we would visit in a few days, when our responsibilities had reached the end of the Retreat.

My meditations and dreams were full of this extraordinary encounter, and the more I processed, the more AY's teachings and prayers became clearer – I knew that a powerful energy was fermenting within me – so my night and day dreams became more lucid. They were filled with dark fleeting shapes – forms of 'the watchers' that had heralded our entry to the Valley of the Baboons – who also brought golden lights that brought awareness to other images, scenes of rituals carried out by apparitions of swiftly moving shaven-headed priests who carried offerings to the Gods and Goddesses, dressed in leopard skins and linen.

These stirrings, and the consistent whisperings of *Ptah will guide you through your Master Thoth* meant that further more profound revelations were imminent. These feelings and the visions of half-lit faces in deep underground Temples fuelled my fervour in wanting to meet the Egyptian Holy Man.

When we finally met the Sheikh, in a ground floor room in a very modest house in downtown Luxor, the room was filled with men drinking Egyptian Tea and smoking cigarettes. The Sheikh, with his penetrating eyes and aggressive Islamist stance, was defensive, and wouldn't illuminate the mysteries for me. Perhaps this was understandable, as he appeared doubtful about the sincerity of my being, was fearful of his own position, and seemed highly protective of the holy spells and secret ways. The Egyptian Mystery Schools were powerful, evocative training grounds for the Priest Class, for those who devoted themselves to the magical ways, and so they were respected. As a consequence, the permeating religious faith throughout this ancient nation was considered incorruptible. The Priests were in life-long preparation, for the sound reasoning of the after-life, and this they upheld as absolute.

After fifteen or twenty minutes of being given psychometric tests, all to prove my veracity, I looked kindly and fully into the eyes of the Sheikh, and suggested through my interpreter that this wasn't what I had come to him for, and that if he wasn't available to me I would respectfully bid him "Good Day!" This seemed to appease him, and he immediately said he would place me in a spell like trance, and then I could ask AY himself for information – WOW!

I quickly agreed, and the Sheikh's son stepped forward, saying that he would also accompany me on this astral journey – whilst he placed a talisman around my neck, to keep me safe and tether me to reality – and I was told his name was Haggas.

A PSYCHIC JOURNEY IN THE VALLEY OF THE KINGS

What then followed was extraordinary for I journeyed into the Valley of the Kings and was shown an inner domed Temple of vast proportion, much bigger than the current Valley structure allows. The walls were covered in elaborate ancient frescoes, layered with powerful spells that seemed like reverberations from another culture – cartouche and scenes from Atlantis itself. The passages were endless, moving at once deep within the mountain, yet also disappearing into the bowels of the Earth, like the famous well deep in the core of the Great Pyramid at Giza – an entry point, or navel into the centre of the World itself.

In the centre of the Temple, on a raised stepped dais, sat a giant Golden Ankh surrounded by exquisite minerals such as Quartz and Diamonds, at least thirty metres in height. These forms transmitted powerful electric rays, derived from the converging magnetic lines of Earth force beneath, and from the Stars above.

The reason for this location, the Pharaoh's Necropolis, also became clear – this was a place where the dimensions of the Earth reached a point of inter-dimensionality. This was a site where a meeting point took place between the seen and the unseen worlds, a type of wormhole, as I could see the Ankh led to star-systems that lay beyond our own galaxy. This was a gate to the world beyond this world. This was a nexus of profound proportion, where the voice of God would whisper into the ear of the one who sees and hears, in order to receive divine unction. This was a trajectory for the Pharaohs to slip through into the after-life, and beyond!

Reeling from this information, I was then taken into the Tomb of Tutankhamun, yet the scene was of a time much before Howard Carter discovered the Tomb in 1921. Indeed, the Ptahhotep or High Priest of the place (like AY) indicated that this was the sixty-fourth Tomb of the Necropolis known as the Valley of the Kings, reflecting the sixty-four strands of DNA possessed by human beings. Yet, within the inner burial chamber, he drew my attention to twelve piles of funeral debris, all neatly piled, and not in the chaotic disarray that Carter hadoriginally found. These twelve piles symbolized the twelve keys to paradise. They indicated the distinct passageways through this City of Life, which created a gradual incline towards the zenith of all human spiritual practice – the City of Light lived in by the **Shining Ones**.

The final key opened a gate that meant one had been formed into the action of a **Shining One** and, as this revelation came, each other key and gate was shown to me in greater detail – an entire initiation process to raise the physical body onto higher and higher octaves, so as to meet the possibility of the final reality, that of Ascension.

Ptahhotep stood before me with shaven head and body, exquisitely draped in linen and the skin of a leopard – the vestments of a high priest – smelling of the attar of roses, and with the love of fiercely penetrating eyes. Behind him, a shining disc shone, configured like the sun, and I realized this was actually his vast and magnificent aura. Each of the twelve Angels of Atlantis hovered in their resplendent Orbs around him. Uttering in a tone of immense kindness, he said:

> *I am the enflamement of Truth.*
> *I am the enlivener of the Living Fire.*
> *I am the eternal force that sparks each cell within your body.*
> *I am the divine breath breathing you into existence.*
> *I am the supernal sound that moves you into creation.*
> *I am the pulse of all actions moving through you, and therefore…*
> **Be the continually evolving 'I AM'**
> *And allow me to burn away all that no longer serves you.*

The Twelve Angels gathered before me and one by one revealed:

- *Live like there is no tomorrow*
- *Breathe as though you have the Universe within you*
- *Dance as though no one is watching*
- *Laugh as though no one is listening*
- *Sing the song of your soul for all to hear*
- *Talk as though each moment were sacred*
- *Smile with the love of an Angel*
- *Think with the grace of Heaven*
- *Feel with the might of the Galaxy*
- *Move with the capacity of the Noble*
- *Love like you've never been hurt*
- *Be kind, even when others may not be*

These experiences, and all the visions that have come since our remarkable encounter with AY, have compelled me to write *Angels and the Keys to Paradise.* This story is drawn by a force so powerful that the dynamism of the keys stretches between the worlds.

So let us unfold this journey together, you and I, that I may serve you with truth and love, allowing you to see what magnificence you are, of what your portents are, and of how creation moves through you – for life is not happening to you, life is responding to the shifts and currents of your thoughts and feelings. You have come from far away to dive into the very centre of creation, and here you are on Planet Earth to unearth what on Earth you want to be.

Namaste

—Stewart Pearce, London 2014

SANDALPHON

SACRED GUARDIAN

ONE

THE KHAT

You have already earned a place in the pantheon of humanity, and so well done! It is now the time to soar into the slipstream, and show all what you are really made of.

– THE EGYPTIAN HIGH PRIEST AY

Sandalphon's amber-filled Archangelic presence protects the first key to paradise known as the KHAT and, exquisitely positioned thus, is venerated as the Angel of Reverence. Indeed, for eternity, Sandalphon's being has radiated rays of loving light and sound,to teach reverence and obedience, for these are magnetic states that allow human beings to yield to the vibration of the all that is Divine.

When we yield to the immensity of Sandalphon's love, we yield to God, and so we give in to that force that is more powerful than ourselves. We yield to a Universe that knows exactly what it is doing, which means we give up our attachments to the temporal, we let go of how things appear on the outside and, instead, become connected with what happens on the inside, within our souls. When we surrender to the Divine, Sandalphon draws the essence of the sacred through our entire human form, and the powerful virtue of reverence moves personal will into union with divine will.

Please gaze on Sandalphon's icon, feel how the force of the dawning sun lights up the Sigil making it spin in your minds eye, thus changing the Chi of your whole being. Sandalphon is the Sacred Guardian of the planet, and therefore also of your body. What does the Sigil make you feel?

The Amber force of this great Angel's reach always moves me considerably, creating a counter-clockwise spin in my Chi and, when I move through this energy transition – the growth sensations of my spiritual odyssey –, Sandalphon always appears in my energy field to help oversee the changes.

The attributes of Sandalphon's power ground me, making me feel once more connected with my Soul' s mission – Evolution, Clear Intention, an awareness of my Planetary Cycles, and Eternal Love. These qualities allow me to feel that unloving thoughts deactivate my connection with the Source. Then, once more, Sandalphon allows me to feel the dynamic by which the universe and the planet are programmed to support me.

ANGELS I HAVE SEEN SINCE YOUTH

I've seen Angels since childhood, and remember well the experience of Orbs and Faeries playing with me. I tried catching their beauty when very young, but couldn't, and yet my soul felt constantly in communion with them. In fact, I can't remember a time when I haven't seen Angels, even though as an infant I didn't know they were Angels, because I saw them as Orbs.

Then, when six-years of age, I remember seeing a vast, vivid presence, gathered around a wrought iron sculpture of a man with wings on the side of a building I was told was a Church. The sculpture was identified for me as Archangel Michael, and before the form was a huge Orb of violet light, which spoke to me, saying: *"I am Michael, and I will always be with you."*

Angels appear to me as naturally as though I'm seeing a human being, or any material object, and yet I know them to be made of intense plasma from the Sun and, over the years, they have become my great friends. A long time ago, I remember them saying: "Don't tell anyone you see us, as they won't understand" and, wow, was this proven to me as a child, particularly when I spoke to people about other spiritual entities such as Ghosts and Elementals. So I learned to be quiet, until now, although I've always felt the close presence of Archangel Michael, mostly as an Orb, and sometimes as a shaft of intense light.

Angels have never taken human form for me, and they don't appear with wings – yet I do see beams of light that filter outwards, almost as though feathers were arising from the intense glow of their energy field. This was confusing as a child, because there were so many pictorial illustrations of Angels as human beings with wings that one was expected to believe in. Yet now, my soul suggests this was simply an easier way for most human beings to understand Angels.

Of course now we have digital photography, providing us with a new perspective of these wonderful Orb Wanderers, and I'm always utterly amazed by their form, particularly when they appear solid, even though I know they are refracting their rays in the most fascinating fashion. Indeed, their radiance gives them life, full of the love and light of eternal wisdom, which appears to flow through them with such infinite ease. They feel to me that they contain the essence of the soul of all souls – the very bliss of life – and I've found out that they are also often referred to by some of the great Mystics of the Christian Church – Hildegard von Bingen and Saint John of the Cross – as Orb Beings of immense light.

ARCHANGEL SANDALPHON

Archangel Sandalphon is similarly an intense but intimate presence, holding this first key to paradise. He was formerly known as the Prophet Elijah. Elijah was seen to possess unbending love and devotion for God and, as a consequence of his obedience, devotion and reverence, Elijah evoked the magical powers of raising the dead, bringing forth fire from heaven, and the creation of ecstatic sanctity. Elijah's discipline and practice gave him the faith and courage to accomplish many great things, or so it is depicted in sacred texts such as the Bible.

As a man, Elijah believed utterly in Heaven and the works of God, seeing the whole of nature as being filled with God's breath or Ruach. This brought his faith to a point of undaunted conviction, and so his was able to command the internal voice of his ego which tested him copiously. You see, the more time we spend with the Holy Spirit, the greater our capacity to focus on love as the only reality that exists. At the end of his long life, Elijah's allegiance to the Divine brought him into intense contact with the ALL THAT IS, and so his Ascension to heaven was formed by a whirlwind that carried his soul's chariot (or Merkaba) drawn by flaming horses into paradise. Thus, Elijah became an Archangel.

BELIEVING IN GOD'S INEFFABLE LOVE

For thousand of years before the Seventeenth Century Age of Enlightenment – a time that existed before the rationale of the mechanistic universe – human beings believed in the ineffable love of God. God was seen to exist in all living things – the earth, the rock, the wind, the fire, the tree, the oceans, and indeed in all animals. Quite literally, a widespread collective belief existed that the planet was alive with God's breath, or the Holy Spirit, and therefore was revered by human beings. Whenever earthlings felt spiritually or physically enfeebled, they would immediately go to God – or to the manifestation of God in the form of Mother Nature. This done, they would receive divine unction.

Through the sensory nature of this experience, the energy of the KHAT (the dense, physical body) was continuously nourished by the *anima mundi*, the animating principle of the Universe, and so this energy was believed to keep alive the body of humanity. As with previous civilizations, the human body was felt to be an opportunity to bring forth the Divine into the very substance and fabric of whom we are in human form.

Regrettably, our belief in the mechanistic universe has led us away from knowing the 'soul' as living deep within our physical body – until this time that is. Through the current arousal of the Divine Feminine, within the consciousness of our planet and its people, and as a consequence of the many changes taking place within the Stars and Galaxy, we are at last waking up to remember the power of this loving force. Now we are seeing consciousness as a non-local field of vast intelligence and, in consequence, we're recalibrating our belief in the KHAT as a body manifested soul.

THE MEANING OF KHAT

The KHAT is an Egyptian word indicating the portal through which the soul is made flesh in physical form. The ancient Egyptians believed the physical body to be a temple where the sacred breath of the HU, and the divine word of God, resided. Therefore, they regarded the body as a vessel for the mystical connection between human and divine, so the key to the KHAT existed to lead one to become purely at one with the spirit of the breath, the pulse, the sensations of the body, and the experience of being within human form – as these were considered the rhythms of universal splendour.

The ancient Egyptian Pharaohs lived this promise, as they formulated their sacred practice in conjunction with the High Priests, of becoming fully present to each of life's actions, whilst focusing their intelligence within the chamber of the heart, and so allowing unconditional love to be the guiding force for each of their intentions. They believed that these were some of the paramount features for living a Godly life on Planet Earth.

The High Priests of Egypt also taught that an over-preoccupation with the KHAT could lead to complex shadow behavior, such as the pursuit of hedonism. They believed this to be so when the individual became fixated by the rapacious desire for more stimuli, for more libidinous physical sensation – rather than by revering the inner world of the soul.

Similarly, in our contemporary life, too many parties, too much stress, too many text messages, too many emails, too much TV, too much sex, and too much 'doing, doing, doing' moves the individual to a point where the life force eventually becomes dull, slowing to a lower frequency, and contorting in times of crisis that lead to disease.

Therefore, the High Priests of Egypt put forward the conviction that, if one could attain physical and psychic excellence, any sickness could be cured, healed by drawing harmony and light deeply into the physical body, so that the KHAT could exist in synergy with the soul body – providing health for the individual, illuminating each choice, and creating heaven on Earth.

They believed that Heaven or Paradise was a place in which life reflected eternity: peaceful, loving, joyous, delightful, positive, prosperous and utterly harmonious. Indeed, paradise is the fundamental place of contentment that we all yearn for. It is a home for all that is loving, meaningful and good – it is where God resides – and as Paramahansa Yogananda wrote:

I wandered through forests of incessant searching, and arrived at the mystery door of thy presence in paradise.
On the doors of Silence I knocked loudly with my heavy blows of faith, and the doors of Space flew open.
There on the altar of glorious visions I beheld Thee, resting.

I stood with restless eyes, waiting for thee to speak, and heard not thy creation-making voice.
At last the spell of stillness stole upon me, and in whispers, you taught me the language of Angels.
With the joyous voice of new-borne freedom, I tried to speak, and the light of your temple assumed a sudden brilliance as you wrote in letters of light:

In my little chamber of quietness, I am always resting. I never speak but with the voice of silence, and so through silence eloquently talk with me using the language of light and love my child.

THE NOISE OF DISEASE CAN BE CURED BY THE HARMONY OF SOUND

When physical malfunction occurs, either through trauma, accident, infection or stress, messages are sent to and from the body, suggesting a level of 'noise' is prevalent, that the harmony of ease has dissolved.

It's pretty obvious, from the enquiry exerted in the field of contemporary complimentary medicine, that there is a powerful relationship between the mind and the body. For example, when we become ill or develop a physical difficulty, we must first check the recent past, and then move back further to the distant past if necessary, to review the a change in lifestyle, a period of worry, an unexpected misfortune, or an accumulation of anger of frustration. The event itself may have passed, yet the emotional impact can often stay with us for many years, ingrained in our bodies, and finally affecting us on a cellular level.

It's not always easy to find the deeper cause of our attitudes and behaviours, yet looking at childhood or the past, through the vista of the Chakras process, often opens understanding for what is actually happening in our body right now. For example, were their particular difficulties experienced during childhood, with strongly attached feeling states? Death, separations, or trauma can leave deep wounds of loss, anger, grief, fear and insecurity. These feelings stay with us creating 'noise', and influencing our actions, feelings, behavior and states of mind pejoratively. It's often interesting to see how many of us arise from unhappy or unloved childhood experiences.

Indeed the quality of conversation once had by our parents always gives rise to the crises we experience in life – perhaps we grew up listening to a dispute about whether they wanted a boy instead of a girl; or we have been caught in a breakdown of our parents relationship leading to divorce; or often witnessed emotional skirmishes. These experiences undermine our sense of the KHAT; they pull apart our sense of security, acceptance and worthiness. These childhood fears become adult fears, and in time they begin to affect our health.

Therefore, if we investigate any illness as arising from emotional disharmony, our spirit arouses the soul to recalibrate its frequency, and the miracle of healing begins. Seven million red blood cells diminish, and are reformed in each second of our lives. Similarly, every seven years, our bones and organs are completely reformed. Therefore, pain, illness, distemper or any malfunction of our bodies can therefore be seen as a message that we have an internal emotional conflict or thought that is affecting our very survival.

This, of course, is not God's way of punishing us for any terrible thing that we may have perpetrated, but rather our own personal functioning creating balance out of imbalance. You see, the human body is divinely self-correcting, with its cells seeking out their own creative solution, choosing the highest vibration for the soul's path.

Magically, sound enlivens all things through 'reverence resonance' and, when the human voice is used to sound the OM syllable or the Heart Vowel AH, healing immediately occurs. Sound arises as pure vibration from the Source, and places us in touch with the purest expression of our good, the highest frequency of our consciousness, the greatest aspiration of our faith, and our most fond desire – for harmony is an agency of healing.

Both the OM syllable and the AH vowel reflect the purest intention within the Universe, and therefore God's love within our hearts, and minds, and bodies. The OM is the *prima mobile*, the calling card of God, and sounding this sacred syllable through the heart means powerful energies open for us, the KHAT force naturally expands, and the energy field of the heart expands five thousand times greater than the brain.

This immediately brings super-coherence to the forefront of our consciousness, aligning the individual to the possibility of wholeness, of being a fully embodied soul. Likewise, sounding the AH opens a frequency to loving intention and, as sound crystallizes intention, positivity floods the physicality of our being.

The Priests and Priestesses of the Egyptian Mystery Schools were preoccupied with teaching how to consciously embody the light of the spirit by using sound, which they believed would allow the cycle of reincarnation to be completed. Enlightenment or becoming a 'shining one' was the super-objective, and any human being who lived consciously, by resolving the unseen, shadow complexes, would literally ascend into paradise forever.

They believed that each part of our body has its own unique function and purpose, and this, they felt, corresponded to an aspect of personality (for instance the feet are where we experience a sense of being grounded, where we experience the ability to walk forward through the consciousness of life). Therefore, if we are experiencing negativity in a particular part of our being, that energy weakens the body, exposing it to vulnerability and stress.

The High Priests particularly believed that the lightness and texture of the skin – the quality of luster that the skin possessed – was an indication of how much the living language of light existed in the physique of the person. They believed that through the practice of using clear intention, the resolution of karma, breathing exercises, sacred prayerful meditation, chant practice, physical exercise, light-filled organic food and fluid regimes – the density of the physical body would transfigure into sacred radiance.

Thus, the individual could become a 'shining one', assisting the dream of the eternal beings of Light to create paradise on Earth.

A BODY FIT FOR PARADISE

Once again, in our contemporary world, there is the belief that the physical body is a vehicle for the soul. Once more, we are remembering the body's form to be made of earth, yet that this form is also enraptured by the Spirit. You see, the Earth bears our foundation, it holds the gene of our creative potential, the original form from which our life arises. Therefore, it is vastly important that we keep the Base Chakra nurtured and responsive – through personal awareness, belief in abundance, transcendent love, the intimacy of close friendships and relationships, and a strong connection with the planet itself, it provides us with a way of truly inheriting the Kingdom of Heaven.

SANDALPHON AS A GUARDIAN OF THE KHAT

Archangel Sandalphon, God's appointed Guardian of Heaven on Earth, oversees our physical presence, assisting us to awaken the inner kingdom of our soul's creativity by creating harmony in our body. Sandalphon teaches us to perceive the outer world as a mirror image of what lies within, and therefore governs the physical realm of the planet, whilst being the loving custodian of our KHAT, as well as indicating what is Divine.

Sandalphon inspires us to engage in the art and celebration of being consciously alive – of creating mindfulness by being present and focused in each moment of life – so that we may ask the most important questions of our journey: Am I engaging in the 'presence' of life with my senses open? Am I weaving together the sacred elements of the earth, water, air and fire – corresponding with the physical, emotional, mental and spiritual energies of my being? Am I truly living a life filled with love?

Sandalphon reminds us that the KHAT brings purpose to our creations, particularly with regard to the quality of our choices, for the essence of choice lies within specific intention. The law of attraction states that: thought creates reality, and feeling actualizes manifestation. Therefore, Sandalphon inspires us to know that living in co-creation with the world of essence is also a key to tune the KHAT into receiving high frequency charges from the Universe.

This magnificent Archangel knows that the cycles of nature are completely interwoven with the quanta of the cosmos, and that when our purpose dwells in the heart as a centre for choosing, the Galactic heart centre also responds, shining openness, and producing abundant flow.

Sandalphon walked with the great Neters of ancient Egypt, the Gods and Goddesses of that antique land, and was charged with the vast spirals of cosmic light, condensed from the Galactic Heart, and drawn from the Source. This vast Angelic being was destined to help draw the energy of Planet Earth into the ascension force of the Galaxy – then and now – and therefore, if we work with Sandalphon, we develop greater respect for our planetary lives, for the spiritual richness of the DNA that flows the fabric of our existence, for the very nature of Pranayama as it runs its course through the neural pathway of our spines, and outwards through our flesh.

For being informed of KHAT means that we experience the physical and spiritual backbones at the very core of our lives. Thence they support our movement, transmitting our sensations, opening our love, and radiating our creations into the world.

THE RIVER NILE AND EGYPT'S SACRED TEMPLES

The backbone of Egypt, the communication highway of Egypt's KHAT is the sacred river of the Nile. Without this great river, its abundant life, broad fertile reach, and sweeping majesty, ancient Egypt would not have existed. The Nile reaches for over four thousand miles, arising from the great lakes of central Africa in the south, to the Delta of the north, flowing in a northerly direction with a power that flooded its watercourse between every June and September – before the great Aswan Dam was built between 1960-70.

Along the backbone of the Nile lie strategically positioned Star Temples that exist as astro-geographical locations for the enhancement of Egypt's KHAT energy. These lode-stones mark a meeting point between Father Heaven's spirit, and Mother Earth's nature, for they draw converging Ley lines into powerful vortices, as well as reining in the astronomy of the Stars. Strategically chosen as they were, each Temple marks a Seal or Chakra for the body of Egypt, the body of its people, and for those who now visit in devoted veneration. The Nile is the central neural pathway for the spirituality, commerce, and body politic of its people.

I facilitate retreats in Egypt, and can vouch for the extraordinary nature of each of these Temples. Ruined they may appear, as you gaze at the body of their buildings, yet at he same time they are fully alive within the holographic light of each location; a light that reflects the soul blueprint of each Temple, a light that is so bright that the Temple's form and presence opens to those who have the reverence and grace to feel and see.

The gracious Nile reflects another great river that once in antiquity moved through the centre of another land of great significance. This land was called Atlantis, and the sacred river was known as Alph. This giant water-ribbon similarly brought great abundance to the fertile nature of the land, and to the twelve communions, each of which had a population of 144,000 people. However, post the cataclysm of Atlantis 12,000 years ago, the river Nile, and in particular the country of Egypt, alongside a number of other powerful locations, was chosen as a perfect place for re-creating heaven on earth, just as it had been in Atlantis. So Thoth and the other Priests and Priestesses led the people forth to these new locations

The lush, verdant soil of the Nile valley allowed the community of settlers from Atlantis, whose intention was to live in profound reverence with the divinity of Mother Earth, to create a powerful bond between the celestial and terrestrial realms of the Universe.

The physical experience of the Atlanteans vibrated through a twelve helix DNA, functioning through each of the twelve Chakras, allowing the people to live to a superlative form. This meant a fully joyous union with the KHAT of their bodies, Mother Earth, and an implicit sense of the Cosmos. They knew they were from the Stars, from other planetary civilizations that existed, and indeed still exist within outer space.

The Angels of Atlantis suggest that there are twenty-four civilizations living within our Galaxy, and that the Atlanteans were easily in contact with these beings – as many of these Stars held in there orbit planets highly familiar to the beings of Earth.

Sandalphon, as the Sacred Guardian Angel of the Earth, also assisted the people of Atlantis, whilst they experienced a way of being that vibrated in accord with a completely different biochemistry from our contemporary molecular status. They lived through sixty-four codons of DNA, whereas we use only twenty codons. They vibrated a Twelve Chakra system, as opposed to the Seven Chakras, and possessed a rare energy that was created and nourished by an octave of spiritual intelligence far surpassing anything we currently attain, except for a few notable humans, such as Ammachi, Mother Meera, HH the Dalai Lama, known as the Boddhisattvas.

These are 'living saints' or illumined ones, who through countless lives have cleansed their karma, and have reached a point of rare, unconditional loving; who, through years of spiritual quest, have sought a point of optimum beingness; who, through disciplined service to the Divine, have achieved degrees of enlightenment that vibrate refined states within human form; who possess extraordinary abilities: to manifest matter from anti-matter, bi-locate, and perform supernatural healing. They live an octave of psyche that has the ability to see beyond the material world of three-D, operating through extra-sensory states we refer to as Clairvoyant, Clairaudient, and Clairsentient.

SANDALPHON AIDS THE EVOLUTION OF THE KHAT

Wishing to evolve through these octaves of sensitivity, and desiring to indicate the wisdom that can be accomplished by using the Keys to Paradise, are the *prima facie* intentions of this book. Living in accordance with Divine Will means that we set a level of coherence within our bodies that brings profound healing to our own being, and to the planet. When we enjoy the coherence between personal and divine will, engaging with each aspect of our lives harmoniously, we resonate our core vibration, drawing holiness throughout our entire physiology, whilst experiencing innate co-creativity with all of planetary life.

Within our bodies lies a potential for this Holy Communion, for when we give our body to the Holy Spirit, to Sandalphon, it becomes an instrument of loving transformation. When we see our bodies as small and vulnerable – when we see them just as a body, and not as a spirit that exists within the mind of God, we become disconnected from the Source that is the fountain-spring of all our lives.

Living within the mind of God means that we are much, much more than what we see – for expanding conscious awareness places us beyond the limits of any ordinary physical law. Living within the mind of God shows us that we are made of quantum force, whereas placing attention on the body as an end in itself means we live life through senseless hedonism, placing a burden on our body, which it was never meant to carry. Whereas a healthy perception of our body means we surrender it to the Holy Spirit, and thus it is used as a transmitter for love.

In order to open our KHAT to the probability of vibrating with divine love, we will engage in your own private KHAT SCAN. This is a review of the whole of your physicality, allowing you to determine the holding points (I use this term rather than the word 'blocks') which cause points of resistance within your physical or emotional body, those contusions which don't allow coherence with the divinity of your core vibration.

By identifying these holdings, one can immediately dissolve the challenge, creating wellbeing and vitality. Pulsing with these qualities means that we cultivate loving flow; breathing with these qualities means we create positivism; and loving with these qualities means we alert the magnificence of serotonin and oxytocin as our aids – these are the hormones we produce in heightened states of consciousness, such as when we are 'in love'.

THE KHAT SCAN

- Make sure you have **Silence, Solitude and Stillness**.
- Move to your enchanted sacred space, whether this be in nature or in your own beautiful home.
- Dim the lights, burn incense, and play sacred music that endorses the vibration you wish to create – all of which consecrates the space with a divine countenance.
- Find somewhere to lie down and feel the weight of your body, making sure that your head is supported by a cushion, and your back long.
- Breathe in the healing light of the Universe, and feel the Prana as a brightly colored light moving through the whole of your body

- relaxing you, and creating stillness… do this three times letting your body sink deeper and deeper into being at ease.
- Then having breathed in, sound *AH* very gently through your heart area, feeling yourself arriving at an even deeper point of repose, in the very middle of your being – in effect in your core signature note. Do this three times and feel your inner being so relaxed that you meld with the Cosmos.
- Feel the gentle flow of Chi or Prana flowing through the whole of your physical body, bringing peace, and creating a divine reverie within the seat of your soul, your Heart Chakra.
- Feel your body opening further, and concentrate on your left foot, imagining a healing orb of golden light hovering in your sole.
- Allow the light of the orb to spread through your entire foot – feel the heat, pulse and light of the orb rhythmically flowing through your whole foot, instep, heel, toes and ankle, scanning for any tensions or holding points. If you discover such, simply allow the light of love and peace from the Divine Cosmos to flow through and heal this part of your Khat.
- From your left foot, move slowly through the ankle into your calf, knee, and thigh, scanning for dark spots or scars of damaged tissue from past trauma. As the golden orb moves through you, feel a heat and hum caressing your limbs into freeness and wellbeing.
- Keep breathing the light of Pranayama through you, and you will sense the vibration of your soul emitting powerful rays through your entire being, in order to enhance your Khat Scan.
- Then go to the right foot and, in a similar way, scan your sole, instep, toes, ankle, calf, knee and thigh – allow the golden orb to peacefully flow through your being, scanning any holding points that may be present. Feel out the points of resistance through the pulse and rhythm of the orb, and then gracefully bring loving coherence and healing to any scar, tension or holding point by breathing Divine light through them.
- When you've reached your pelvis scan your loins, your reproductive organs, your bladder, your rectum, your colon – shine the golden light of the orb through these parts of your being and, if you find a holding, allow the light of love and heat to flow and pulse through your being.
- Observe how the first and second Chakra rotate freely in response to the spreading light of the golden orb – possibly flowing in a clockwise direction.

- Then move to your middle abdominal area, scan the kidneys, spleen, gall bladder and intestines. What do you observe?
- Bathe this part of your body with the humming melody of the golden orb, as Sandalphon suggests this is the darkest part of the body, and intend there to bring the light of healing to this part of you. Observe the way the golden orb suffuses this area of your body, producing the warm pulse, and resonance of your signature note, caressing and bathing this area of your being. See the third Chakra spinning in your light body, rotating with the supreme health that is your core vibration.
- Now move upwards into your liver, your lungs and heart, scanning this area carefully, bringing all the organs, muscles and tissue into complete coherence with the symphony that is the divine you, filled with the melody of your love and joy. Caress your heart Chakra with the melody of the golden orb, humming and bringing joy.
- Then move upwards into your throat, seeing it as a passageway between your body and head, between feeling and thought. Caress your throat Chakra, feel the humming melody calming and easing your Thyroid, as this is an important conduit for the healing welfare of your whole being.
- Gradually move into your mouth, your jaw, your tongue, your ears, your eyes, and through the brow Chakra into your brain, bringing light and the melody of infinite caress to heal any point of resistance.
- Move into the *corpus callosum*, into the very centre of your brain, spreading the golden orb and healing warmth of the coherence melody throughout your whole brain, and directly into your crown chakra.
- Pause for a moment, and then breathe the golden Orb light through the whole of your skeletal structure, feeling love seep deep into your bone marrow.
- Hover in these sensations reviewing the journey that you are taking, and perceive any of the holding points that you've noted. If there are any, simply regard them as needing to move back into the core vibration of you. Then you will amplify their healing by the hum of the golden Orb, healed by the exquisite melodies of the chakras in balance and harmony
- Pause – collect your thoughts and complete your KHAT SCAN by feeling immense gratitude for the wonder-filled health that you experience right now, drawn absolutely from the Source.

THE LIGHT BODY

Fully living light within the KHAT, in a world that is overly fixated with three-dimensionality, can be challenging. Living in a world that is drenched in toxicity, is even more challenging, particularly as there appears to be little or no evidence of Spirit in the wasteland of GM Foods, the over-usage of fossil fuels, and the tragic use of nuclear fusion.

And yet, although these challenges exist, other intelligent systems co-exist alongside the techno-field that spans the Earth. These neo-paradigm systems are alternatives to the overly cerebral left-brain world, and are created both as a means, and as an opportunity to magnetize towards us an even greater field of consciousness, the non-local domain of the Spirit.

This field of consciousness is much bigger than any other, and is entered through the portals of consciousness we are beginning to resource, even though our ancestors were extremely accomplished using them. For example, through disciplined Meditation and in silence, we may penetrate the realm of feeling and intuition with relative ease, and thus connect with the many beings of light that populate that world – the Angels, the Devic Kingdom, and the Elemental spirits of Gaia.

Within each of us there is a silence, a silence as vast as the Cosmos,
a silence where all things meet.

– DR DEEPAK CHOPRA.

THE STILLNESS OF THE CORE

Our quest is to find that silence deep within each of us, for this is where God resides. At this still point lies a gateway into infinite consciousness, into the morphogenetic field, into the place where God dreams creation into existence, and it is our job to find a way into this space by increasing the light field of our KHAT.

Illumination has its beginning in the stillness of Meditation, because Meditation draws the fibres of our soul together. Meditation allows us to truly listen on a much deeper level than when we just hear. Meditation brings a rare degree of light to our consciousness, and this deepens our relationship with the sacred. Illumination is like a spiritual laser that cuts through the resistance to the liberation beyond. Illumination allows us to recognize that we are living in visionary times, and need to cultivate visionary faith, for illumination cracks open the mind, and lets the light of the free shine through.

Luminosity is the free flow force of the mind that influences the world in a positive way. Over the last twenty-six years, the planet has been flooded with spiritual light, focused by the disciplined Meditation of the many Light-workers who have been awoken by the vast waves of astronomical change created within the Universe, and gifted to the Planet. These inter-galactic changes of circumstance heralded the events of 11.11.11 and 12.12.12, which were the luminous portals that gave us such richness on 21.12.12 (12.21.12 in America).

These were the shafts of luminosity that keyed open genetic codes harboured within our cellular intelligence – codes that opened stored wisdoms concerning the experience of living within this Galaxy, and of how life on this planet has been for time immemorial. These are the ways by which we may use a new compass to take ourselves forward, beyond the historic data offered by the world's intellectual elite.

This luminosity allows us to see that we are living a process of celestial light speeding-up. So the light of the Source becomes brighter. This is the light that will prize open the remaining aspects of our shadow complex, alongside the patriarchal establishment that holds such tight control through its guard-dog of fear, a beast that snarls and barks against the illumination of love. Yet still, love waves us through the spaces where cruelty exists, for it unites us all as one.

When we see the light inside us shining outwards, creating a holy communion, we radically alter the way we are – for no longer do we see each other cast in darkness, separation and aloneness. Instead, with the light, we see alongside us Angelic Beings waiting to anoint us, sharing the elixir that soothes us in the recovery of our divine inheritance. Living thus, we alter the belief that we are disconnected from Divine Mother, we see the Cosmos as one living whole, we dispel the notion of competition in support of collaboration, we radically turn to love for succour, and we revolutionize the mistaken belief that we think solely in order to stay alive.

Inside us are countless generations of ancestors, suffused within our hundred trillion cells. These beings learned to overcome challenges and survive terrible storms, and similarly, we too will find a way to endure, to revere obedience, and also rediscover insight, hope, courage, humility, grace, faith, joy, charity, patience and love. All we must do is prepare the inner terrain of the KHAT as a worthy vessel for our soul, in co-creativity with the soul of the Cosmos.

SANDALPHON'S TWELVE HEALTH REGIMES TO INCREASE THE LIGHT OF THE KHAT

- Remove dead animal flesh from your health regime, as it holds no light.
- Select whole, natural foods from the core of the food chain, such as beans, seeds, fruit, vegetables and grains.
- Eat fresh vegetables, mixing raw food with lightly steamed vegetables, and ideally straight from the plants source.
- All living beings flourish through love, and so choose foods that aren't chemically produced.
- Do not microwave food, and bless food before eating it.
- Dispel coffee or tea from your health regime, substituting these compounds with herbal teas, and place quartz crystal in your drinking water, making sure the quartz is charged with love, and that the water is pure for drinking.
- Breathe light into your body, and use light-filled visualization techniques.
- Meditate at least once a day for twelve minutes, and draw the light of the cosmos deep within your cells.
- Chant the OM at least once a day for thirty singular chants, focusing on the **love** of the Cosmos vibrating within your heart.
- Diminish negative emotional behaviours and reactivity – instead focus on responsive grace-filled contact.
- Practice compassionate acts, non-judgmental behaviour, forgiveness, and the unconditional love of inclusivity.
- Embrace Mother Nature at least once a day

These **Light** measures will assist your attunement with the great note of your individual soul – a note that reverberates throughout the Galaxy. Each element within this practice will help you restore the music of the Earth's soul, and so your KHAT will resonate through the energy field of all living beings, entraining all to absorb more light – and allowing any darkness to be transformed into the light.

Let us draw these finite thoughts through the infinite space afforded by the stillness of the meditative process. Let's embark on an Archangel Sandalphon Meditation.

SANDALPHON'S KHAT MEDITATION: BLENDING WITH THE SOLAR DEITY

- Find **Silence, Solitude and Stillness** in your sacred space, whether this be a meditation sanctuary, or in a specific place in nature.
- Burn incense, ring a bell or singing bowl, play sacred music, switch off cell phones, or any communication technology, and find a comfortable chair in which to sit, or sit cross-legged on he floor.
- Feel your spine as fully aligned as possible, establishing your KHAT energy, and imagine an amber laser light shining through your entire spine.
- Follow the amber light down through the base of your spine, through the chair, the floor, the building… into the basement, the earth's crust, the soil, the clay, the stone, the rock… and deep into the bedrock, into the very womb of Mother Earth.
- Sense how Mother Earth receives your laser – your call of gravity. She is always present with unconditional love, we just forget her.
- See from the end of the deep amber, further light filters, growing like amazing roots, magnificently extending throughout the vast rock deep beneath you.
- These are the light tendrils of your soul's incandescence, the light of your KHAT seeking out connection with Mother Earth, and immediately feel her loving elixir nourishing your physical form.
- Ask Mother Earth for a gift, a vision, a sensation – and then siphon the energy up through these tendrils and the laser of your pranic-cord, into your heart's secret chamber. Extend upwards further, all the way through your spine, up and out through your crown chakra.
- Feel the amber light extend even further, upwards into the expansion of your energy field, and then above tuning into Father Heaven and the Sun – the Solar Deity.
- See amber light tendrils extend upwards and outwards from the top of your pranic cord, literally expanding into the vastness of the non-local spiritual intelligence of the Cosmos.
- Notice that, as these lines of force extend upwards, they also begin to absorb light from the Sun, a golden nourishing light that moves in a downloading fashion, into your entire KHAT, and your physical form.
- Check your spine is fully aligned, and feet or coccyx touching the ground, then breathe in the Golden Light of the Solar Deity seven

times, allowing the light of the Sun to collude with the amber light of Sandalphon's strength.

- See the Golden Light of the Sun permeating through the whole of your being, nourishing every single cell with the energy of this Great Star.
- See the golden light reach the hundred trillion cells of your body, allowing the light to disperse any negativity from your body, healing any corruption, resolving any conflict, soothing any woe, whether it be conscious or unconscious.
- Then chant OM seven times, allowing the vibration of the AUM to resonate throughout the entirety of you KHAT.
- [Pause]
- Observe the unique vibrational force moving through you, as the Great Star Centre of the Universe makes profound connection with you, with your KHAT. This will nourish you and allow a sense of divine bliss to be bestowed upon you.
- Pause… and be still feeling each sense providing you with the unique information of this harmony

The KHAT as the first key to paradise now needs interconnectivity with the eleven other keys, and so we will move to the REN, the second key to paradise.

GABRIEL

DIVINE MESSENGER

TWO

THE REN

Vibration is the core of Cosmic Consciousness,
and goodness is movement in pulse.

– JOSEPH RAEL (BEAUTIFUL PAINTED ARROW)

Archangel Gabriel protects this great key to paradise, for REN is the power of the all, flowing through the vibration that shimmers in the energies of Sound, Colour and Light, bringing forth manifestation into being. Thus, with celestial grace, Gabriel brings us to divine insight, as a vibration directly from the Source, which we then dispense through the experience of our lives, for Gabriel is ubiquitously present at each act of conscious creation within the Galaxy. This is the essence of REN, for it is comprised of the very nature of potential being.

Gabriel's infinite intelligence knows the vital force that lies within the power of light and sound, and how nothing lives through form without vibration. This is the divine vibration that brings forth all from the void, through the cascading rings of magnetic fusion, into the kingdom of life on Earth – thus Gabriel flows with the grace of the eternal.

For time immemorial, Gabriel has been known as the Divine Messenger of Creation. This beautiful Angel of Grace explicitly knows how to use vibration to help name things, and so assists by bringing into existence each aspect of planetary life that arises for divine function. The Divine always manifests through vibration, firstly by producing the nature of essence, and then through the act of naming, for without an object's name, form remains unknowable, and mysterious.

CREATION THROUGH VIBRATION

The ancient peoples of our planet believed that all creation was brought about through the vibration of sound, interplaying with the light. Indeed, they believed that sound accomplished the making of all things, bringing the Earth itself into being, and that original sound still moves through every aspect of creation. The ancients ones believed that this animating principle was the sound of God's voice.

An echo of this still occurs today, for in certain areas of the world

Shamans hear the sound of Mother Earth. Furthermore, their sensitivity means they possess the ability to know each plant, each tree, each rock, each waterhole and each animal by their sound. They hear the note of each living thing, and pronounce its identity as being drawn from the very essence of vibration – as though identity were elicited from an unheard and utterly divine chorus. For example, have you ever heard what crickets are hearing, beyond their extraordinary chirruping?

Similarly, human beings have always dedicated their voices to the veneration and glory of God as the prime creator. Through praise, petition and participation, we have given up our voices in devotion, for "In the beginning was the Word, and the Word was with God, and the Word was God", and God said: "Let there be light and there was light!" The stories of the 'big bang' of creation exude from every culture, by which we may begin to apperceive the vibration of the great OM, the seed syllable of creation.

THE ORIGIN OF SOUND

Many years ago, I met a leading Aramaic scholar at the Sorbonne University. This learned gentleman had spent a period of study in the Vatican Library. Once, whilst reading papyrus scrolls originally found in the early 1950s in the Qumran Caves of Israel – a discovery called the 'Dead Sea Scrolls' – he found a scroll which he translated and read: "In the beginning was Sound, and the Sound was made flesh."

Isn't it wonderful to know that God named man through sound, so that man's flesh would ring with the resonance of divinity, and that man has identified God for centuries using different tones. Indeed, the very word 'human' is drawn from ancient sonic glyph or word, connected with the spirit of God. In the East, the sound of the outpouring breath is known as *HU*, and is known as the spirit vibration of all sounds or words. In Sanskrit the *HU* means 'the breath of spirit', whilst in Arabic the *MAH* means 'water'. Furthermore, in eastern mysticism, the word HUMAN illuminates the two ideas within the character of humanity: HU means 'God', and MAN means 'Mind'.

The two words then fuse, indicating that God lives within all beings, and that it is through nature that God is known – the nature and essence of humanity, the natural world, and the extraordinary Galaxy. The Bible says: "Except a man be born of water and spirit, he cannot enter into the kingdom of heaven". Without the REN of vibration arising through the spiritual impulse of the Universe, with God's breath descending through the water of life, human beings are merely barren KHAT.

The ancient Egyptians celebrated this teaching through their sacred and secular sound making. They injected the resonance of their sacred harmonics with magical ingredients that created the power to levitate stones, produce light with which to see, as well as to heal. They believed that, through sound, the triple function of the eternal, the universal and the individual was suffused with past, present and future. They believed that the Divine Now or Holy Instant was the only true measure for recognizing the core nature of vibration, and that within this force lay the blueprint of all things, the essence of their Gods and Goddesses.

This lambent intelligence can be seen in the story of Genesis when God spoke: *Let there be light* and there was light! Before this there was no light to see form through, and after this salutation to creation, the Almighty continued naming throughout the whole of creation, whilst simultaneously bringing form and nature into existence. God then commanded Adam to identify each living organism, so that each and every form was named.

Likewise, in the Egyptian Creation Myths, Ra spoke at the beginning of Creation, and bid the earth and the heavens to rise out of the watery waste, and in this brightness the Neters – the Gods and Goddesses – appeared in magnificent Light.

THE CELESTIAL SHAMAN

Gabriel as a celestial Shaman comes forth like a dove of peace yet with an administering boldness, caressing each of our chakra, as well as naming their purpose. Touched so, we become blessed in the arousal of our spiritual path, we discover that love and compassion are the only way forward, and so our initiation is announced in each breath of Heaven.

This divine breathing – this sacred sounding – draws the essence of the Holy Spirit the *HU* deep into our beings. It is the jet stream for the Angel's progression and, when its mighty wind blows our path, the essence of devoted creation lightens our path with REN.

The stories of Gabriel are rich and magnificent, as we see in the messages given to Mary and Elizabeth in the New Testament. They illustrate Archangel Gabriel's ability to manifest 'annunciation', to be present at epoch making moments in history, for both women are explicitly told about their veneration in bringing forth sons that are pre-destined to be extraordinary people. As we know these two beings became Jesus and John the Baptist. Similarly, fulfilling this sacred role, Gabriel appeared to Jesus shortly before his final hour on the cross, to strengthen the resolve of this exceptional man, the Son of God, for his inevitable crucifixion.

Gabriel is the Archangel that selects souls from heaven to be born in human form. Ancient fables, such as those within Kabbala, suggest that Gabriel spends nine months with each unborn child, informing the spirit about what life the newborn will acquire, including how the soul will be engaged in certain karmic lessons during incarnation, only then to silence the child before birth, by pressing an Angel's finger on the child's lips, so producing the cleft below the child's nose.

Gabriel's other legendary task was invoking the Koran for Mohammed. So this great Angel is seen aplenty, providing celestial support through the vibration of REN sound. Gabriel's mighty force, full of divine insight and supernal grace, illuminates the conviction of the sacred messages we receive directly from the Divine and, through these teachings, we are brought back into closeness with God.

In this closer perspective, Gabriel is the governing spirit of the water element – the waters of feeling. For we are born of water, and when we fully accept the vibration of our soul's transcendence within our KHAT, we inevitably feel a profound movement back to a wholeness of being, held within the vibration of feeling created by the spirit within.

REN is the spiritual essence of a person, and at core, is the soul – the soul that we are at this time opening, for a new world awaits us as our minds and bodies are healed by love.

THE REN'S AFFIRMATIONS

REN is the song of your soul.

REN is your spiritual note or sonic glyph, grounding you to bring forth effervescent truth.

REN is the vibration by which you manifest your heart's desire through your name.

REN is the quickening you feel as you immerse yourself in the expression of the sublime unconditional love of your heart.

REN is shimmering when you feel connected with your heart as a repository for your soul's essence.

REN is your soul made manifest through your name, and the echo of I AM THAT I AM.

REN is made fully present in the moment you feel the ecstatic vibration of your note, creating a field of force about you, that elicits holistic harmony.

REN is the reverberation of that vibration which creates a field of limitless potential.

REN is the vibration of your signature note made manifest for the whole of creation.

REN is the vibration that chooses to serve God for. when we seek the Source, we choose the path of God's greatness within us.

REN is the constant movement towards a new vibration of bringing forth our grace in the world, and receiving joy as we live the sovereignty of our beauty.

FINDING THE SONIC VIBRATION OF THE REN

- Seek out **Silence, Solitude and Stillness** in your meditation room, or a natural setting, making sure all communication technology is switched off, so as not to disturb you
- Burn incense, play sacred music, ring bells or play singing bowls, and light candles – all with the intention to purify the space by consecrating it as an altar.
- Sit with your spine as aligned as possible whether this be in a chair or cross- legged.
- Imagine that you have a silver laser beam of light moving through your whole spine – the pranic cord – and visualize it moving down through the base of your spine, down through the building into the soil beneath Earth's surface, the clay, the stone and the rock, deep into bedrock, deep into Mother Earth's womb.
- Notice how she receives your force, and grounds you to allow the gravity of and form of your KHAT to be stabilized. This is very important, as it will allow you to feel magnetized to the weight of the Planet, into the warm embrace of Mother, who is always present with unconditional love.
- Then reverse the polarity, drawing the silver laser up from the Earth's womb and through your body, taking it right through your spine, and then seeing it leave through the top of your head out

into the space above, seeking out a connection with the vastness of Father Heaven.

- Then let all the breath empty from your body, through your lips. Feel the need to breathe, and draw in the silver light of pranayama through your nostrils, illuminating the whole of your interior, so that each cell appears to be a star.
- Try to breathe wide and deep, to avoid pushing the air into your belly, which creates tension. Truly open the width of your rib cage where great support lies – support for the breath into positioning your voice.
- Try doing this three times, letting go of all the air, and then breathing in, so that the breath fills your being effortlessly, and really touches deep down inside you.
- When you feel flexibility with the rhythm of the breath, sound *HAW* three times through your pelvis, on three separate breaths, feeling the vibration fill the whole of your being.
- The *HAW* is the Earth element, and so will ground your vibration. See it as a red-brown vibration filling the whole of your pelvic area.
- Then sound *HOO* three times, on three separate breaths, through your solar plexus/heart area. This is the water element, signifying the vibration of your emotions. See the sound as a silver light brushing against the shores of your ribcage.
- Then sound *HOW* three times, on three separate breaths, through your throat area visualizing a beautiful blue light, for this is the centre of the air element, representing the vibration of mind.
- Then sound *HEE* three times, on three separate breaths, through your head centre. Visualize white light filling your upper body, for this sound represents the inspiration of pure spirit
- Then sound *HAA* three times, on three separate breaths through the centre of your heart. What colour comes to your being representing this, your core vibration, your heart's note, the song of your soul?
- To finalize sound *ZZZZZZZZ* through your spine, and you will feel the vibration flowing through the whole of you, particularly reaching a vortex in your heart.
- Return to sounding *HAA* three times, on three separate breaths through your heart, then rest.
- Soak in the vibration of stillness, feel the currency of such peace moving through you.
- Feel the vibration of your soul, for you have just found the song of your soul.

- [Pause]
- Feel the weight of your being, the depth of your breath once again in your stomach, and the amazing stillness in which your vibration soaks.
- This **Stillness** is vast. This **Stillness** is the soul of vibration, the vibration of soul.
- Remember this vibration and slowly open your eyes, reviewing the journey you've just taken.

THE SIGNATURE NOTE OF YOUR ESSENCE

We are all unique, and our paramount vibrational force comes to a point of coherence through our own individual note. This is the 'signature sound' of your whole physical being: distinctive, rich, unique and therefore completely unlike any other vibration.

Your note is God-given as the sound that sits at the core of your being. This is the resonance that reflects and amplifies who you truly are – this is your **Soul**. The soul is a super position for all spirit, and arises as a fragment of God, a divine spark created especially for your life, arising from the furnace of God.

Once you have identified the note of your vibration, you will feel harmony moving through you, and a strong sense of connection with all that is Divine. You will feel as though you have come home to that deeper part of knowing yourself, where all trivia just falls away. This is a place of far greater knowing than anything you may have experienced before. It is the kingdom of your essence for, when we sound this realm's vibration, we create the experience of our 'sovereignty'. This means we create a connective resonance between the King/Queen archetypes at our core, for sovereignty indicates that better part of you, that is strong and noble, and wise.

Sovereignty, in the temporal world means that we possess a balanced state of awareness in the expression of our personal power, which is qualified by the way our gifts are received. Thus we achieve social recognition and are elevated, because the excellence and integrity of one's character are fully noted.

Sovereignty, from a spiritual perspective means we align our personal will with Divine will, and so are anointed by God. When we hand back our personal power to God, because he/she knows what he/she is doing much better than we do, we are truly blessed. John Donne described this as: *I am a little world made cunningly of elements and an angelic sprite, which in truth is God's blesse'd preserve.*

The purpose of the REN, the purpose of vibration, is to name that part of yourself, which gives birth to the very best within you, that part that God intended for you to express. This means the sound you emit gives consciousness evidence of itself, and so the knower becomes known to the self, as when consciousness gives witness to its voice.

Human beings are not alone in producing signature notes. Every solid form existing in the three-dimensional world has its own specific and distinctive note or vibration, which in turn creates its own unique resonance and frequency. This is within everything – a tree, a table, a glass, or a human body – all are in a perpetual state of vibration and movement. The matter we perceive as solid is merely a cloak for energy.

All matter is made of atoms, through which electrons spin around a nucleus, and so produce vibrations. Simultaneously as vibration occurs, sound is emitted, travelling in the form of waves. This happens at varying speeds – electrons that spin fast produce high notes, whilst those that spin slowly produce low notes. These speeding sounds are measured by units referred to as Hertz, which occur in cycles per second.

The vibration of any object also creates a resonance frequency. Imagine striking a note on a piano: initially one hears the pitch of the note, and then the resonance produced by the other notes tuned to the same frequency. This resonance is like an echo effect, created as the sound waves oscillate through disturbed air. When the other notes sound, it means they are in harmonic synergy with the initial note, and are therefore referred to as harmonics.

DISCOVERING YOUR NOTE

In the same way, we can find the sound of our own note – just as the resonance of the other piano notes echo the initial note – we can also 'play' or vocalize a note that echoes all of our constituent parts and, therefore, it becomes a reflection of our whole physical self. This note is our significant signature.

Imagine that your whole vocal range is stretched in front of you on a horizontal, like the keyboard of a piano, then find the middle of a piano's keyboard – the note 'middle C'. The bass notes below middle C are the low notes, and the treble notes above middle C are the high notes.

The notes of a piano are organized into octaves, the word 'octave' arises from the Latin meaning 'eight', and refers to the eight-note sequence upon which the whole of Western Classical music is based. It is known as the diatonic scale: CDEFGABC.

If you were to play the treble notes in the higher octaves of the piano, you would hear higher pitches. Similarly, if one were to produce high notes with the voice, the resonance would primarily appear in the upper body or head. Conversely, if one played only bass notes on the piano, one would need to strike the keys in the lower octaves.

When comparing this to the human voice, if you produce only bass notes, the sound would arise from the lower part of the body, the stomach or pelvic area. However, if you imagine two hands playing the piano keys astride both treble and bass, one would experience a harmony of sound, reflecting the potential full range of the instrument. If we relate this to your voice, all we need to do is to convert the horizontal plane of the keyboard into a vertical plane, and place it alongside your spine, and a potential range of full sound will be opened in the body.

Our spines are the major conduits for the energy in our body. They are the neural channels that transmit information to every cell we possess, and this happens in less than twenty milliseconds. One brain cell reaction can spread to hundreds of thousands of cells in a period of time that is ten times shorter than it takes for the human eye to blink. If we imagine our voice in the centre of our spine, near to the heart Chakra, the spine will vibrate the signature note of our whole range.

Try sounding a *HUM* in your forehead on a fully supported breath sustaining the sound. Try not to sing on a vibrato, but just sound the note at the top of your speaking range. Feel the sound vibrating in the bones of your face, just between your eyes. Then, on a sustained breath, support the *HUM* down through your spine, as though the spine were an elevator shaft – you will possibly cover two octaves, maybe three, although this varies person to person.

Complete this exercise to the lowest comfortable note you can sustain, and if you need to, recover the breath, but try not to lose the position of the note. You will feel this sound flooding through your solar plexus, vibrating a note with a resonance that feels of the Earth. Imagine it to be red-brown in colour, just like the soil. It's important not to push the note down or to tighten your throat in any way, as the slide should be easy and flow freely.

This discovery exercise can be very enjoyable – it's fun to feel the tickling resonance zooming down your spine. Use the visual image of an elevator moving down its shaft as suggested, and see its colour like the light-force energy of your breath awakening the sound. If it is difficult to see a colour, imagine that you are seeing it as pure white light.

Keep practicing this until you feel comfortable with the skill. Then try directing the *HUM* to a point just in the lowest part of your sternum. It is important to keep the breath free, expanding the physical flexibility of the vibration. When you have vibrated the sound from forehead to sternum, you will feel an amazing vibration throughout your torso. Place your hands on different parts of your upper body just to feel the vibration touching down.

When you reach your breastbone, imagine lips appearing from your chest, or see a beam of light emerging from the center of your heart Chakra. Then open the *HUM* into *HAH*, and you will feel your note. The sound will feel as though it's arising from the centre of your spine, and spreading from that nexus through your entire being. This is rather like dropping a stone into the middle of a still pool or pond, and watching the ripples move to the edge of the pond.

With a little practice, you will feel the whole vibration and resonance of your voice arising from this centre. The upper and lower vibration of your voice, the harmonics, will come together to a point of clarity, and so you will feel the significance of your KHAT or physical presence sounding its signature note, as an individual means to feel the REN of your soul, vibrating through your whole consciousness.

Keep practicing this simple sequence and, as repetition is the Mother of skill, you will eventually feel the sound to be a distinct, weighty and true vibration of the whole of you. When this happens, blend the *HUM* into a *HAH* and then into a spoken count, from one to five. When you do this, it's important not to sing but speak, and you will feel the core power of your being arising from your note's vibration. You will feel a sense of sitting in the middle of yourself.

Now use an affirmation, such as: "I am powerful, I am powerful, and I will use my power for the greater good!" and while the sound of this note is fresh in the vibration of you, ask yourself a few questions like:

- What colour is the sound?
- Which word adequately conveys the power of my note?
- Which sound most represents my signature's essence?
- What feeling does this vibration give me?
- Can I feel Gabriel bringing intuitive messages through my note?
- In which life-situation do I most need to draw this sound?
- Am I fully expressing my power in life?
- What does my Sovereignty feel like?
- In which situation do I most need to live this vibration thoroughly?
- Am I fully accepting my magnificence?

- What is going to be the result of feeling my full resonance?
- Who do I feel is using the magnificence of their note?

Noting and remembering the answers to these questions will help you to easily recall and repeat your signature note, particularly as words anchor sensory states in our being. These behaviours will truly create a dynamism that hitherto you had possibly not opened yourself to.

THE DYNAMIC ENERGY OF YOUR VIBRATION

Finding your signature note, the REN vibration of your truth, will startle your heart into its own awakening. Thus, you will be able to further develop the different aspects of your being that vibrate with the:

Earth: Balanced Grounding

Water: Honest feeling

Air: Thought Elasticity

Fire: Spiritual Illumination.

As sound crystallizes intention, you will feel a remarkable power exuding from your whole physical geometry, which will create a window for your soul to be fully communicated to the world.

Exploring the potential of our vibration – exploring the vibration of our voice through our signature note – leads us to express feeling states that have often been held back for some time. Please do not hold these from expression, for feeling is the language of the soul, and so enliven your whole process by working through the emotional memory. Yet do find a skilled practitioner to help you do this if possible.

Ultimate healing occurs when we remember that all conditions are temporary in our evolutionary process. I firmly believe we are living a cosmic experiment that matures the soul through the physical/emotional exercise of living daily life on Planet Earth. When the going gets tough, we must muscle up our souls, and develop individual will as a potential strength for us to truly muster the vibration that makes us the Master/Mistress of our destiny.

By finding your signature vibration, you will also find your blueprint, freeing up your feeling capacity, and opening your soul's expressive power. For within your voice lies the blueprint of your humanity – the song of our soul. Experiencing your note will sensitize you to other people and, when you hear their psychological blueprints, you will ultimately be brought to greater empathy, richer relationships, and an ability to explore your creativity in a much more diverse way then before.

At the same time, vibration on this level makes us more discerning, so that if we are around people who do not vibrate truth, we discern how to interface with them, or we may move graciously away. The question is: do you want to be around positive or negative vibrations?

Exploring the versatility of vibration through vocal expression can be extremely liberating, allowing unforeseen possibilities to emerge. Through crystallizing thought in sound, you will feel as though you are more fully emitting your creative intelligence and vibration in the world. For once your voice is centered in your note, resonance will emerge from different areas of your body, depending on the level of thought or feeling you are using.

For example, did you know that there are different energy centres in your body from which sound organically emerges? These energy centres hold thoughts and feelings directly connected with sense memories, and provide us with profound ways of expressing our integrity, just as you've experienced by tuning into the elements in the section above.

THE PELVIC FEELING CENTRE – THE EARTH

Breathe in fully, both wide and deep, and sound *HAW* on your lowest comfortable note, but without pushing down. Imagine red-brown earth deep in your pelvic area, the pit of your stomach. The immediate vibration will be one that folds the earthy core of you into itself. The feeling will be very 'impressive', rather than expressive, as though you are touching the deep core of you.

This will create impact in that deep part of your substance which life sometimes dislodges us from. This is a sound we primarily use for deep visceral issues.

Try saying something from this part of you, such as below; just check you aren't 'pushing down':

"I'm deeply affected by this moment!"

> *What does it feel like?*
> *What emotions arise for you?*
> *Does this feel free or blocked?*
> *Does this sound bring with it sensory feedback?*

I believe we return to this sound when experiencing deep emotional states, such as grief or sorrow. We use these emotions to go deep into the pith of whom we are, to recalibrate ourselves in moments of profound life change. For this reason, if you are harbouring unexpressed feelings from your past, drawing sound from this part of you may bring emotional memories to the fore that truly need releasing. Expression is the key liberation to our destiny.

THE HEART TRUTH CENTRE – THE WATER

Take a deep breath, wide and deep, and sound *HOO* through the upper abdomen or heart area of your being. You will feel the sound to have weight and gravitas. You will sense how your heart opens to the resonance of its truth. You will feel its full glory and richness, and this will make you feel strong and courageous, leading you to an experience of your archetypal sovereignty.

Try saying something on a fully supported breath from this part of you, imagining a beam of light emerging from your heart, or as though your heart centre had lips, opening to express this point of vibration:

Come, be with me in love and power!

This heart-centered vibration is often taken from us by powerful people in our lives – folk that we've given our power to – for, if truth be told, the traumas can feel as though they've been done to us, even though we've also unconsciously chosen to give power away. Therefore, we may see that the disempowerments are ways our soul learns about love and joy: Why on Earth would the suffering have occurred? Control dramas can of course be initially rather daunting, until we size up to the covert psychology of the one who perpetrates them. Centering your sound vibration in your heart brings you fundamentally back to you, it returns you to your power, and ultimately this will give you strength, magnificence, and glory as illuminating convictions.

THE THROAT EXPRESSIVE CENTRE – THE AIR

Sound a note through your throat on the vowel *HOW* using a fully supported breath and making sure your breath is wide and deep, full and free. Imagine the colour of light blue. This colour will help you to create a truly open resonance for the vibration to have impact, both internally and externally.

If this is challenging, imagine a favorite drink or ice cream sliding down your throat. Then sound a yawn, opening your throat by fully dropping the back of your tongue.

We tend to live our lives in major Metropolitan cities with our tongues permanently raised against the back of our mouths, as a result of the physical and psychological tensions we experience. We close the sensing organ of the tongue against the rear of the mouth, the soft palate, because it shuts out any unwanted intrusion, rather like a trap door. Try lifting the back of your tongue tightly against the roof of your mouth, at the rear, and say *GE, GE, GE* then yawn. Then release the tongue completely, and on a gentle *GE, GE, GE,* you will feel sound flooding through your body, whereas before it was trapped.

The vibration will feel soothing, sensual, gentle, wooing, rather like your being intensely confidential, or engaging in pillow talk. Try saying:

How wonderful it is to feel such joy!

The vibration will be soft, easy and soothing, inducing Alpha Brain Rhythms in the listener. So, if you are attempting to relax someone, think light blue, and centre your vibration in this way, and the listener will become highly sensitized to your state.

THE CEREBRAL THINKING CENTRE – THE FIRE

Breathe wide and deep and sound *HEE* on a note in your forehead. See the vibration as being white or pink, and your whole head will be filled with the sound.

Try speaking a phrase here, such as: *Today's weather is sunny and clear!*

You will possibly feel the vibration as a rather 'objective' sound, a vibe held in intellectual deliberation, or for imparting information alone. This sound occurs when we are engaged in the exchange of informative or cerebral action. The energy is electrical and rather fire-filled, so you won't feel it as magnetic, as you did when positioning through the heart or throat.

The Cerebral Centre is one we use most in our metropolitan communities, where we spend our lives usually rushing around, moving through, alongside, or indeed over a harsh terrain of concrete. Of course, this 'doing' complex affects our minds, bodies and souls, and so our sound is under-nourished by the breath, and becomes thin, reedy or metallic. Be reassured, if you use the throat opening exercise I gave in the Throat Expressive Centre section, you will release the nasal twang over a period of time. Of course, this all depends on your level of individual awareness.

Practice all four of these centres for vibration, and you will begin to discover the full extent of possibilities lying within your signature note. When your breath and throat resonator are free, you will certainly feel yourself opening a much greater vocal range, allowing you to express REN more purposefully, and with greater depth. Your voice and whole being will feel more relaxed, more open and therefore more creative. Then notice the effect your voice has on other people, and you will experience a sense of honouring that you hadn't felt for some time.

The purpose of our lives is to give the very best of ourselves, to give from within, and these questions need to be asked: What do you wish to give? What do you wish to become? Life is not a journey through which to discover self, but a means by which one can create oneself anew. Healthy human emotionality expressed from the heart is the leading edge frontier of human evolution and, therefore, the first advantage to re-create oneself anew.

Conscious awareness of the REN, means we render ourselves to the manifestation of our life's passion and, where there is passion, there is purpose. If we trust in our heart's ability to transmit our soul's purpose, we begin to create our wildest dreams much more easily. Whatever moves us to create passion in the next moment of life, whatever makes life exciting, let's follow that passion no matter how crazy it may seem.

THE CREATION OF SACRED FORM FROM REN

Our bodies are cosmic listening posts in a vast ocean of vibration, and so our beings are water-filled landscapes that receive vibration directly from the Source. All is vibration and so, throughout the sands of time, we have built Temples, Cathedrals and Pyramids as vibratory chambers to harness the fundamentals of REN energy. Ancient peoples knew that the experience of highly attuned REN moved them to open the multi-dimensional aspect of their consciousness.

Holographic thought is where the vibration of light takes over from sound, and so the mind gives way to the mystical. Here we open a dimension where oracular messages are received from the Gods or the Neters. This is a portal to the limitless space of everlasting knowing, where true insight is formed, where matchless beings like Archangel Gabriel literally hover – for the intuition of the mystical is a superhighway where the Angels roam.

In Ancient times, crystals were used to amplify this level of consciousness, within the great Sacred Star Chambers of our planet and, as crystals are powerful electro-magnetic transmitters, they allow us to interface between the mortal and the divine. The Great Pyramid was one such temple complex, which was filled with crystals at strategic points, permitting a unique vibratory meeting point between the infinite and the finite, between mantra and mind.

Goethe is reported to have said that: *All architecture is frozen music,* and I believe this means that the geometry of a building's form holds a force of vibration. When this is venerated by astro-geography, by geomantic earth energies, by the shape of the building's sacred geometric precision, by the devotion and love pledged by human beings who worship there, the Divine is enlisted to resonate specific celestial vibrations through the building.

THE ARCHITECTURAL RESONANCE OF YOUR BODY

Just as the superstructure of a great building such as Shakespeare's Globe Theatre, the Taj Mahal, or the Temple of Karnak supports the infrastructure of living vibration that takes place within it, so our bodies need a similar support, to allow their essential vibration full resonance. In this regard, our spines are the central support structure for the skeleton, muscles, joints and sinews, and therefore hold form as the core pillar of our body Temple.

If we achieve an open free-flow physicality where our central column is aligned yet flexible, we also generate a sense of personal power which exudes a powerful vibration from our body that is felt by all. To achieve this, firstly we need to bring attention to focus on our physicality and, when we've achieved this, we discover what is most 'noble' about ourselves; we tune into what the highest choice could be for ourselves, and we make profound choices about our thoughts and feelings, our dreams and sensibilities, our sacred and profane visions.

Shakespeare's Hamlet said: "*What a piece of work is man, how noble in reason, how infinite in faculty, in form and moving how express and admirable, in action how like an Angel, in apprehension how like a God: the beauty of the world, the paragon of animals.*"

The resonance here is consummate, for it identifies a unique model for embodying the vibrational form of our being, our human-ness. To understand more about the amazingly magnanimous nature of your body – how you can desire to keep healthier and more vital, how you can help to create more meaningful relationships through the Angelic substance of your being – as a 'shining one', let's tune in further to the core of your REN nature.

We once believed, before the mechanistic interpretation of the Universe, that man is a microcosm of the macrocosm, and therefore the foremost creation of the Divine in God form. So, in ancient Egypt as in Atlantis, and as in Medieval Europe, it was believed that human beings were made from a confluence of the divine elements: Earth, Water, Air, Fire, and Ether, the latter being God's breath.

Furthermore, it was believed that integrating these forces from the very inspiration of life would move us into the force of the Divine Muse. From this supernal position, we could acquire Angelic status – we could light up the world.

ANGELIC LIGHT PROCESSES FOR OUR HUMAN REN

- Check you are in a space where you can stand comfortably, and place your feet in a parallel position, about six or eight inches apart.
- If you feel that this parallel feet position draws your knees. together, open your toes and feet slightly. However, make sure your feet are not too wide apart or too turned out, as this will rotate your hips, and push your pelvis forward.
- Rock backward and forward over your heels and toes until you reach a comfortable position balanced through each foot between your heel and toes, and through your insteps.
- This will feel slightly strange if you are used to standing with your weight over your heels. When we move forward in life from a habitual position, we tend to move forward with our weight backwards, which is very retroactive. In other words, we carry the unresolved nature of ourselves (our baggage and unexpressed feelings) into the future.
- Try walking around, feeling how freeing it is to carry your weight forward. But do check that you do not look like a leaning tower of Pisa, and use a full length mirror to help see your physical alignment purely achieved.
- Check that your knees aren't braced back, with your thighs and calves tense. This is something we often do when we are nervous or anxious, rather like gripping onto the floor, with our toes clawing the insides of our shoes, as if holding on for dear life. Just let go and relax. Our knees are powerful movement terminals in the body. Our knees allow us to flow with a yielding force (imagine yourself kneeling in supplication to the highest divine authority), as well as providing us with the greatest pliability – the knees are the shock absorbers of our bodies.
- Check that your pelvis, the moving centre of your physicality, is 'tucked under' without clenching your buttocks, knees or thighs. Simply place the backs of your hands against the lower spine (the lumbar region) and move your hands downwards, tucking or tilting your pelvis under slightly, to lengthen the base of your spine. Many of us arch in this area, which shortens the lower back and tightens the muscles of your pelvis, and butt, throwing you off centre.
- Feel the length of your spine leading upwards from its base, with the lumbar region open, the middle and upper spine lengthened, and your neck very long. Finally, check the position of your head, with neck long and not pushed forward.

- Check that your shoulders are not rounded or braced back, and try bringing your hands up to your heart centre, with fingers just touching, and elbows pointing outwards. This will allow you to feel open, rather than constricted through your heart centre.
- If you can, check this detail whilst looking profile in a full-length mirror. You should be able to see your shoulders balanced over your hips, and your hips over the centre of your feet.
- Take a deep breath in, widening rather than lifting the breath into your body. See the breath as light filling the whole of your physical form, feel the vibration filling your body as though your whole being were a temple. See your body as long, and wide, and sovereign. Sound *HAA* several times right through the centre of your heart, and imagine a beam of light shining out from you, indicating openness. This will help you focus the whole of your vibration to your heart, the seat of the soul.
- Close your eyes for a moment, feel the stillness, and notice the deep presence in the vastness of that space – this is you soaking in Soul, and surrounded by the vibration of the Angels.
- Bring the purest intention into your heart, and immediately see it as a beautiful silver-white Orb. Fill this Orb with your **Love**.
- Sound *HAA* three times gently, holding love in this beam of consciousness, and notice how each time you do this, the Orb becomes bigger and bigger, until at last it extends all around your body, as though you were within the Orb.
- Notice how each of your Chakra have become open with the power of this Light, this Chi.
- Keep holding the purest intention, the **Love** of your life in your heart, and see it radiating out into the world affecting all of the people in your life. Start by caressing your intimates, and then moving to the people you casually brush past in life
- See them all through the Divine Perspective of the Universal Mind, filled with love, achieving great magnificence in their creative energy. In turn, as they receive these rays of loving intent, feeling caressed by them, notice how they are also experiencing the increase in their energy fields. Then see how rays of loving force from the power of their hearts also extends outwards from their increased energy fields to people.
- As they touch these people in their lives, notice how that network of light expands even further, through the lives of all these people until you reach beyond in ever-resonating circles of light and joy

- Review this vastness: you have just developed a **Network of Grace** that expands to an ever increasing large group of people. You have just acted as a Human Angel, borrowing the inspiration of the great Archangel Gabriel, who in the status of the Divine Messenger brings information to each of us.
- You have just sent love and light to hundreds, thousands, then millions, then billions of people.
- Pause and evaluate the enormity of what you have just achieved.

Archangel Gabriel and the Angels of Atlantis pour such loving praise on the action you have just given yourself to. The Ancient Egyptian Gods and Goddesses also look upon your gifts as the action of an Angel. Therefore, both parties are in absolute conviction that the REN of the holographic mind has just been opened with such purity of force, and highly commend you for embracing this key to paradise with such purity and beauty.

You have just opened the lives of many to the infinite glories of the universe. The glories are always present, for that is the nature of the universe. It's just that they were always simply awaiting your, and others', acceptance.

Perfection is your eternal residence, to which the universe is programmed to return you,and, whenever you may deviate, this will be so. Now you are returned to the richness of what the Angels wished to communicate, because this how you are loved and cherished.

RAZIEL

DIVINE MYSTERIES

THREE

THE SHEW

Until we have seen someone's darkness,
We don't know who they really are.
Until we have forgiven someone's darkness,
We don't really know what love is.

— *MARIANNE WILLIAMSON.*

Archangel Raziel stands in profound vigil over this key to heaven, for Raziel is the portal-keeper of the Divine Mysteries and assiduously checks our bio-identity credentials in order for us to enter into these halls of divine wonder. It is in these halls that the code of your soul is played as an infinite symphony, and so it is here that the light and darker aspects of the human countenance is recorded.

Raziel's particular angelic duty is to overshadow the power of these mysteries, as a consequence of the acutely sacred nature of their stored energy within the Halls of the Mysteries, suspended as they are in the plasma of the Cosmos. These halls are similar in part to the great libraries of our three-dimensional world, except that they are supernal repositories with no material books. These templates contain the record of God's eternal truth and ultimate wisdom, akin to the cache of infinite consciousness used in the movie 'The Matrix', where descending and ascending logarithms of light hold the entirety of eternal consciousness.

However, through the refractions of eternal light that bring us into this time frame, something is stirring within the templates of infinite understanding, which brings us to a different account of ourselves.

What is significant for us at this time, as we regard these mysteries, is that we are living through an acute period of sacred recalibration. We are living within a vortex that configures as a spiritual revolution. We are living a time when the divine mysteries of the soul are being made available to us in an unprecedented fashion. We are experiencing a force of light that particularly manifests transparency and honesty, as it passes through our lives with a velocity that is super-sonic.

This force arrives like a fountain of Divine will to bring us to a greater sense of grace than hitherto experienced, because this force is generated by a Galactic heart, which was ignited by unique astrological configurations occurring within the cosmos, and which beats a pulse that brings forth echoed memories of another time.

The ancient Atlanteans believed Raziel to be the Angel of Illumination, who, standing on the heights of Mount Poseidon, dispatched the secrets to all mankind, whilst shining as an iridescent ray filled with love and faith. They believed that Raziel was one of the major conduits through which the secrets of the soul's code were carried directly from the Divine One to the people. They believed that God had assigned Raziel with this highly significant role before the beginning of time, as a keeper of soul's knowledge, because this Archangel carried a grimoire of divine wisdom in one obsidian ray of its being, and a crucible of eternal life in another ray.

Raziel, as the champion of the mysteries, opens our consciousness to the possibility of all that is hidden, and therefore all that is seen. Cabbalistic legend has it that Raziel offered the book of knowledge to Adam and, in envy, the other Angels took the book and threw it into the deepest ocean, at which point God ordered Rahab, a primordial Angel of the deep, to restore the book to Adam. It is from this Book of Raziel that Noah derived his plans for the Ark, and from which Enoch garnered most of his wisdom.

Enoch's tome became known later as the Book of the Keys – the bio-computer keys to our consciousness within this time zone. At the end of his long life, Enoch notably became the Archangel Metatron, who continues to teach us the wonders of cosmology through the instruction of the great white brotherhood of light.

The mysteries draw forth excellence in all of us, for the mysteries bring us to an account of ourselves. Releasing the negativity of damaging concepts that we inflict upon ourselves, is quintessential, not just because they create feelings like hurt, fear, worry, guilt, anger, judgment, sadness or depression, but because they aren't true. The mystery initiations of the spiritual path take us on an odyssey to literally surrender all fearful thoughts and feelings, and instead we must allow them to be substituted with God's way of being.

When we unpack both our personalities and souls, when we allow the totality of our interior world to be investigated and cleansed, we become as pure as God first intended. Being refurbished thus enables us to see the unconscious shadow aspect of our mind, in all that is hidden – so we see all our unexpressed truth from the cradle to the grave – then measure ourselves in ways that God thinks of us, for we are here on Earth in his image, and nobody else's.

As we wander through the shadow-lands we can see a myriad of experiences that have been stashed away, with measures of fear and anger – diluted then condensed, stirred then anesthetized. The chief of these is the emotion of fear, which so often arises when we perceive threat, and which also brings sadness, fright, dread, abandonment, panic or acute stress along with it

Then there is anger, which is related to one's interpretation of being denied, offended, wronged, or diminished. Anger rears its ugly head via retaliation, and is so often squashed down because of the social mores associated with negative expression, only to emerge during times of immense stress.

The Persian mystic poet Rumi suggests that we see all these dark shadow emotions as friends:

The Guest House

This being human is a guesthouse.
Every morning there is a new arrival.

A joy, a depression, meanness,
some momentary awareness comes
as an unexpected visitor.

Welcome and entertain them all!
Even if they're a crowd of sorrows,
who violently sweep your house
empty of its furniture,
still, treat each guest honourably.
He may be clearing you out
*   For some new delight.*

The dark thought, the shame, the malice,
meet them at the door laughing,
and invite them in.

Be grateful for whoever comes,
because each has been sent
as a guide from beyond.

– RUMI

UNPACKING THE DARK ROOMS

The negativity we experience arises from over-identifying with our material plane of existence, rather than yielding to the divine-will we all yelled into existence, when first we sprang from our Mother's womb.

When we over-extend ourselves within the mortal plane, which works at best as a parade of perceptions weathered by our thwarted wants or needs, none of us appear perfect. However, when we surrender the misperceptions of our own self-account, and meditate for God's account, we recognize how perfect we are all the time. Prayer and chant return us to the spiritual plane, they ground us within the spiritual vibration, and so we re-perceive ourselves as perfect creations of God. For this is who in essence we truly are.

Deriving energy from the Source, participating, petitioning and praising God is something human beings used do, when the collective belief exists that the world of Mother Nature is teeming with a force of unlimited, unchangeable, and all-nourishing energy.

Since medievalism this force has been known as the anima mundi, the animating principle of the universe – or pranayama, chi, ki, sechem. It is the divine elixir from which we are all derived, and is a force that brilliantly flows as an unfolding creative possibility full of love and joy. If we identify with this spiritual force rather than with the material reality enlightenment occurs. If we keep thinking and feeling that we are separate from this force, we become bound to rely on the perceptions of others, rather than on God's.

However, children of God, and not one of us is more brilliant than anyone else is. Your mistakes, or other peoples' opinions about your failures, do not in any way, shape, form or limit who you truly are, or indeed what is possible for you to achieve.

THE NATURE OF THE SHEW

The ancient Egyptians believed the SHEW to be their ally, because, as the shadow, this is a force that profoundly teaches us through the experience of adversity. The SHEW shows what can once more be uplifted into the eyes of creation, for to truly sense the mystery of the shadow is to touch the soul of heaven.

Furthermore, to name the SHEW is to identify that aspect of self that dwells far from the light, and therefore it is the part that most desires reintegration with the light, with the collective soul. It is that part that yearns to marry with the light, to cease the enigma or confusion, by once more healing the duality between the seen and unseen, the conscious and the unconscious, the light and the dark. The SHEW works in our personal and collective consciousness to illuminate what we have left in the darkness of life.

To confront the shadow, requires humility, vulnerability, authenticity and transparency, and when our newly acquired visionary capabilities enable us to be clear sighted, we pass through the darkest valley of the shadow, because we see the light on the other side. The visionary does not look away from the shadow but through to the light beyond. Jesus said: If you have faith as small as a mustard seed, you will move mountains. It is this precise vision that we need at this time, not rose tinted and closed to delusion, but transparent and open to scrutiny.

Thought and feeling are powerful living energies whose repercussions are metered out throughout our local and non-local space, just like the echo of a wild shout in the canyon, or an idly thrown stone into the abyss below. Every thought arises from a cause that creates an effect, and so if we litter our lives with undisciplined thinking we automatically create a deterrent for any creative success. Thinking and feeling negative shadow complexes, sabotages our creative energy within the dynamics of the Universe.

Carl Jung suggested that:

One doesn't become enlightened by imagining figures of light, but rather by drawing the light into the darkness, and creating a light filled consciousness.

As we identify, purify and redistribute the energy of our shadow from within, more space is created within our cells for the light to reside, and therefore the spinal column opens to the process the Ancient Egyptians called the Osirification process. Similar to the Kundalini awakening of Eastern Yogic philosophy identified in the second century BC, the Osirification process locates spiritual energy, the Sekhem at the base of the spine, and then draws this elixir all the way through the spine.

This is known in Egypt as the Djed. The drawing up of this energy, the subsequent opening of the neural pathways in our spine, triggers a growth in each of the seven Chakras or Seals, and in the Far East this is conceptualized as a coiled serpent in the base of the spine, which climbs the spine using its pranic fire, and purifies the entire energy of the being. We can see this in the Caduceus symbol.

THE OSIRIFICATION PROCESS

The Osirification process has a parallel with the Seven Holy Sacraments of the Christian Church, the Seven Chakras of Hinduism and Buddhism, and the Sephiroth in the Kabbalistic Tree of life. Indeed, the Christian Sacraments are bathed in the light of the Christ, as we see from the record of his life in the New Testament, for the sacraments are an outward visible sign of an inward visible grace. They are:

Baptism – gaining identity within the Church.
Confirmation – gaining membership within the Church.
Communion – participating within the Church as a mature witness of the faith.
Confession – renouncing any sins, or atoning karma.
Marriage – finding union with the Christ, through self-realized love.
Ordination – accepting responsibility for teaching the mysteries of the faith.
Extreme Unction – receiving the blessed anointing of the Christ through the instrument of the Holy Spirit.

The Holy Spirit is the subtle force that connects us with the universe and brings us life, through Sekhem or Pranayama.

DISSOLVING DARKNESS FOR LIGHT FIELD EXPANSION

Our shadow can be a portal to the Source, and so together we are going to identify the those compound aspects of the SHEW, then release the cause and effect of its energy. By doing so you will identify your Karma, the emotional themes that stop you from living the free-flow existence of your light, and you will see how the Karma we entered this incarnation to dissolve, can be released.

Interestingly, karmic holding points can be seen held within the plasma tissue of the spine, and it is these karmic lesions that form the causal reasons for why we reincarnate life after life to seek healing. Once this is determined, we truly have the possibility of creating an advanced light field emission such as:

1. When we have dissolved 85% of our darkness we begin to work on a collective level, with sacred perspective, and so we create change on a Global scale.

2. When we have dissolved 90% of our shadow we begin working on a Galactic level.

3. When we have dissolved 95% of a shadow we begin working directly with the Source.

THE MODEL OF THE SEVEN DEADLY SINS

A classified model was identified by the early Christian Church, in the form of the Seven Deadly Sins, to express the nature of the shadow or SHEW, and I mention it here because you may wish to use the idea as a parameter for your own personal discovery, as you calculate your own SHEW or sins.

Within the other great faiths, there are alternative beliefs in relation to Sin (a transgression of a moral law), and are observed as cause and effect in reference to Karma (what you sow you reap):

1. WRATH – anger
2. AVARICE – greed
3. SLOTH – laziness
4. PRIDE – excessive high opinion of self
5. LUST – overwhelming desire
6. ENVY – jealousy
7. GLUTTONY – consuming immoderately

The SHEW's voice will always allow you to know when you are not aligned with your core vibration, because the SHEW is desirous, and hardwired for catharsis. You see, the shadow is the evolutionary journey of your soul, that part of your being that willed itself to meet again with the lighter side, and so to become an interlocutor between the conscious and unconscious. When this meeting occurs we are reminded to see conflict as a pathway of self-discovery, as a way of not judging, but of embracing the SHEW.

Just as Jesus didn't banish Satan but asked the dark one as a representation of the SHEW to get behind him, or in other words to protect his back. For, if we look on the face of the SHEW with faith in the miraculous, we create a conduit for profound healing. Indeed, to look on any situation with faith in the miraculous, means we look with the eyes of God.

If we can remember that we are spiritual beings, and that only the Source can be our mainspring of power, because the Universe is made up of elements that inherently support our life, then we truly begin to think with the miraculous, and in a miraculous way, for the Universe is calibrated to manifest through us the highest possible creative joy, and the greatest love.

Albert Einstein, one of the genies of the modern world, said:

There are only two ways to live your life. One is as though nothing is a miracle. The other is as though everything is a miracle.

To align us with the miraculous, Jesus gave us the seven Beatitudes or Blessings. They were given during his Sermon on the Mount, and help us to see with ultimate conviction what light shines beyond the darkness, and therefore the force that we can rely on as the power we can bring from beyond, to literally back up our lives with divine sustenance.

By saying the Beatitudes, by feeling the resonance of their blessing within us, by living their beauty and content, we literally create a trajectory through the collective thought, through the collective SHEW to the very consciousness of Christ himself. Therefore we become Christed, we feel the love-light circuitry at the centre of the Universe begin to shine through the whole of our countenance, and so we see the gates of paradise.

THE BLESSINGS OF THE BEATITUDES

Blessed are the pure in spirit for theirs is the kingdom of heaven.

Blessed are they that despair for they shall be comforted.

Blessed are the humble for they shall inherit the earth.

Blessed are they who hunger and thirst for abundance for they shall be filled.

Blessed are the merciful for they shall obtain mercy.

Blessed are the pure in heart for they shall see God.

Blessed are the peacemakers for they shall be called the children of God.

Blessed are they who are persecuted for forgiveness sake, for theirs is the kingdom of heaven.

– THE GOSPEL OF MATTHEW, CHAPTER 5.

(You will see that some of the seventeenth century language has been translated into a contemporary meaning to allow us a greater connection with the convictions that lie within each aspect of faith for the miraculous.)

SHOWING THE SHEW

What do you believe are your shadow aspects of the SHEW – these are your Karmic patterns?

List three things that summarize your life lessons:

1._____

2._____

3. _____

What are you prepared to relinquish into Divine Will?

1._____

2._____

3._____

Once your Shew or Karma is Atoned, Expiated or Reconciled, what is it that you feel your life will provide revelation concerning?

1._____

2._____

3._____

ANGELIC MEDITATION FOR THE RELEASE OF SHEW USING THE VIOLET FLAME

- Find **Silence, Solitude and Stillness** in a sacred space – whether this be your meditation sanctuary, or a natural environment of great beauty
- Light a candle, burn incense, ring a bell, play a Crystal Bowl or music – consecrate the space with your own specific intention to embark on this unique journey
- Switch off all information technology
- Feel your spine is as aligned as possible, so as to open the Djed force, making sure your whole body is fully composed
- Use a Mudra bringing your thumb and forefinger together – this aligns your body with powerful planetary correspondence
- See the Pranic cord as a silver light moving through your spine and then down through the varying levels beneath you – the building, the basement, the earth, the clay, the stone, the rock and into the womb of Mother Earth
- Feel how she is present with you, holding you in unconditional love, and as you feel your breath free in your body, moving as the tide moves at a beautiful shoreline, notice how Mother Earth's rhythms also join with yours
- Sound a *HUM* deep within your pelvis three times, and then reflect on how the soul sound of Mother Earth moves through your body
- Sound *HAW* three times, and then be still for a moment, noticing how your rhythms, pulse, and breath synchronize with Mother Earth's circadian rhythms – you will feel the presence of soul at this moment
- See the silver light of the pranic cord once more rising through your body and passing out through the top of your head, shooting off to be in connection with the Planet Venus
- Sound a *HUM* high within the upper part of your head three times, and reflect on how the solar force of Father Heaven moves through your body
- Sound *HEE* three times, and then be still feeling how the rhythms of Father Heaven – the planets and the richness of life within the soul of the Solar System are moving as waves through you, vibrating all the way through you
- Feel how the force of Father Heaven and the strength of Mother Earth meet in the centre of your body, within your heart, and therefore within the seat of your soul.

- Sound *HAA* three times through your heart Chakra bringing the sound of your soul fully into the presence of your being
- Sit in Stillness feeling yourself soaking in soul, and drawing to you all your Spirit Guardians who wish to assist with the uncovering and releasing of your SHEW
- Feel Raziel the Angel of the Mysteries particularly close to you, called by your faithful intention to move beyond the limited locale of material consciousness, and into the much larger world of your spiritual consciousness
- Feel Raziel helping you to identify certain aspects of your Shew, using the Showing Your SHEW list compiled earlier
- Chant *OM* three times shining the light of your Heart Chakra into the space before you, about seven feet away from your being, and imagine this force as a wonderful Green Orb floating in the air before you
- See this Orb as a focal point of your whole being, whereby every part of you is refracted in its light, a focusing of your Heart's Council and an emanation of your Soul's Intelligence
- Imagine the Green Orb transforming into a beautiful Violet Flame.
- Chant *OM* three times again fanning the flames of the Violet Fire, and seeing the energy elongate into a pillar of flaming Violet
- Then Pause and feel the healing that will occur as a consequence of this Sacred Action
- Meditate on your SHEW lesions deep within your Djed, and see all the shadow reaching a point of culmination, then say this prayer:

PRAYER FOR THE RELEASE OF KARMA

Dear Angel Raziel and Spirit Guardians,
Please hear my prayerful plea as I beseech healing from the Violet Flame.
Grant me the clarity of your wisdom, the peace of your love and the courage of your guidance.
Please hear my supplication as I acknowledge the gift and service of my destiny, transmuting and cleansing all parts of my ancestral and personal karma forever.
Please release………………………………………………..
Please allow Divine Love to flow freely through my conscience purifying any pain, and let my essence be as clean as when my Soul came first from the Source.
Lift my heart into the beauty of the Universal Mind, and the

Miraculous Source, and please 'Oh Winged Orb Messengers' of God overshadow me with your Divine Love of Universal Truth, showing me the way of light-filled love.
    And so it is.
    Amen.

- Feel Raziel's magic healing all the way through your being, in each holy instant.
- Notice how the light in the Djed of your spine is becoming brighter, and that each lesion is releasing itself from your body, so that eventually you feel washed clean, as each cell is cleansed by the ritual of the Violet Flame.
- Breathe in the pranic cord from Mother Earth and Father Heaven
- Hover in this delicious space of light, and say this affirmation three times:
  > I'm free, I'm light,
  > ALL IS WELL,
  > And I'm a perfect match
  > For my core vibration!
- Be aware of the fact that the entire communion of the Angels of Atlantis are surrounding you, giving you their love, as they know how you have gained great knowledge in transcending the ritual choices you have made.
- Please say this prayer to finalize the meditation, seeing yourself surrounded by light, the light of your soul in correspondence with the celestial presence of the Angels, and Spirit Guardians:

A PRAYER TO SEAL THE DOOR OF REMEMBRANCE

Dear Angels of Atlantis,
You are always beings of beauty in my eyes.
You are always words of love in my ears.
You are always a sense of glory in my body.
You are always a thought of joy in my mind,
You are always a feeling of compassion in my heart.
Please let me remember the pure sacred lineage of my being,
As I remember my soul's memory, and before the darkness came.
Please let me dispel any darkness from my energy, and
Close the door where evil dwells.
Please let me proclaim the loving, naked truth of my soul,
Knowing it is as sweet as Angel's song.

Thank you dear Angels.
So let it be,
Amen
OM

Then take time to pause, recover and reflect on this amazing process.

Spiritual cleansing is a divine corrective for anything that may have happened in your past, in this life or before. If we can supplicate through prayer, our love is always accepted, and through the expression of love, miracles occur. It is the sacred expiation of any negative programming you may have received from the parental, social, educational or cultural influences that will create the miraculous.

Utilizing the Violet Flame Ritual means you can literally erase the tape, having fully valued the teaching each experience has offered you, and having seen the promise of a new life before you. The story, the old script, was just a story or a script. The question **now** is what are you going to choose? Before you were held by the woundology of the past. Now, spiritually maturing into a new life, you can surrender the old so that the Universe may tell you a new one.

This is true transcendence. This is where there are no denials. This is where your whole countenance becomes as of a child of God, utterly connected to your core vibration, living in the celebration of the exquisite sense of **now**, and fully aware of carrying the perfect model of the Universe within you. Living thus means you are naturally entitled to miracles, because a miracle is what you are.

Once more, you will find yourself speaking with God's voice, because you've reconnected with God's choir. Using his voice means you are a host to God and not a hostage of your Ego. This means that you will be the recipient of endless creativity, power, and abundance. Therefore, feel yourself singing a different melody, a different song, and thus you will be reconnected with the Source of the great I AM THAT I AM.

Mantra of the I AM THAT I AM

I am Love

I am Creation

I am Divine Will

I am Divine Love

I am Divine Voice

I am Divine Vision

I am Divine Wisdom

I am Divine Soul

I am Lunar Female

I am Solar Male

I am that I am that I am

I am Spirit and Essence

And we are all one

HANAEL

SACRED WARRIOR

FOUR

ᛏHE SEKHEM

The day will come when, after harnessing space, the winds, the tides, gravitation, we shall harness for God, the energies of love. And on that day, for the second time in history of the world, man will have discovered fire.

—TEILHARD DE CHARDIN

Archangel Hanael, the glorious Sacred Warrior, governs the fourth amazing key to paradise known as the passion of Sekhem. This is the life force that weaves, waves and sears through all the currents of our existence, caressing us, encouraging us, or warning us when change must happen. For if we are truly to be the people we want to be, if we are to evolve at this time of immense opportunity, we must recognize that change is a constant flowing river, and that permanency is but a phantom of illusion.

If we can allow ourselves to soul-surf through life seeing that every thought, word and deed is in creation flow, not resistance, life truly becomes the marvel that the Source principle anticipated it would be for us, within and without, even before we came into incarnation. From spiritual essence, we come forth into mortal manifestation.

The Universe is encoded with the evolutionary breath of creation, aided by the great Archangels such as Hanael, who is also known as the Angel of Courage. You see, the Universe flows with infinite ease, and so there is no up-stream in the glory of this cosmic gathering of forces. However, here on Planet Earth, we are taught that 'there is no gain without pain', that effort fulfills all desires. This immediately moves us to expect difficulty, and so we start pushing against the current of flow in order to achieve the basic tasks of life. Then, if we are fortunate, we recognize the need to unlearn this myth, and instead yield to the Divine flow of the cosmos by moving 'downstream'.

The Universe is completely self-correcting, and possesses its own GPS system. Just as we have variants concerning our geo-physical location, so does the Universe. Do you remember the last time you were given an instruction by your car Sat-Nav, and having turned direction incorrectly were repositioned a few meters down the road? This is how the Universe works, for it is centered in a non-material state of perfection. The Source is your eternal residence, and living within this state of grace is the way to feel enlightenment surging through your life force, which in ancient Egypt was known as SEKHEM. If you observe your life, notice how whenever you have succumbed to deviation the Universe always brings you back to you.

Hanael, whose name means 'the glory of the Divine', assists by re-orientating us, particularly when we have deviated from our soul's path. For every major lesson, every major teaching that our soul learns whilst on this trajectory of Earth, life was decided before coming into flesh. In this, Hanael is particularly sensitive to our needs, shining forth a ruby red ray. This was first brought through the inspiration of creation by the planetary intelligence of Mars, to help us be firm in the direction of our choices. Thus Hanael marshals our life force – the force that is the Sekhem – which flows directly from the furnace of creation within the Source, and is dispensed within the intelligence of purpose, courage, zeal, steadfastness, bravery, independence, stamina, and will.

HANAEL AS CHAMPION

Governing this particular key of paradise means that Hanael brings to account the way we muster our own life force. Therefore, Hanael champions our spiritual muscles to be in peak condition. If we pledge ourselves to Hanael, beseeching this Angel to truly flex our spiritual muscularity, we are always introduced to a new way of being where our lives become more co-creative within this great playground of the soul. Each mindful choice and loving action moulds the whole fabric of our physical reality.

You see, the Angels in this context teach us that life on Planet Earth is actually a cosmic experiment, and that this is the only planet of choice in the whole of our Solar System. Being here on Earth means that we are engaged in a binary system of choice, where we operate through the law of two, believing that nothing is singular, everything is plural. What this means for SEKHEM is that we are constantly moving between the universal poles of love and hate, of thought and feeling, of light and dark, of masculine and feminine – the list actually reaches off into infinity – until we become part of the Universal Mind, and no longer operate through duality.

For this express reason, Hanael's presence advocates a sense of purpose, for between the poles of contrast arises a stillness which brings us to a rare point of definition. The stillness creates a furnace, from which the blazing qualities are ignited, of bravery, courage, championship, sovereignty, loyalty and victory, for these are some of the cardinal virtues of this sacred warrior Angel, who also emits peace through every breath:

At the still point of the turning world,
There the dance is
Except for the point, the still-point,
There would be no dance of opposites, and there is only the dance.

– T S ELIOT

The mountain champion you see in the Icon at the beginning of this chapter epitomizes the Sekhem of Hanael whose courage, determination and purpose lives by the motto: "the main thing, is to keep the main thing, the main thing" – a concept that allows us to codify our behaviour when all else appears to fall away. For until thought is linked with purpose there is no intelligent thought.

The fortitude of Hanael's Sekhem is brought to pass by the red ray of our Base Chakra, which is the bio-computer from which we express our core identity. This energy centre allows a powerful code of balance to be lived because it returns us to the point where know who we are; yet who we are, and who we wish to become, are in constant need of definition, as we move through planetary life oscillating between the poles of our reality.

The Earth, like our Chakras, is encoded with creativity and perfection. For how does a small acorn become a mighty oak, how does an egg give life to a small bird, or a bud flourish into a tiny flower? Each thing is codified by the master principle of the Matrix, which stabilizes us – in spirit, there is no lack, only abundance. In spirit, there is pure Sekhem, which ultimately means love. When we make a vote for love, we live with the knowledge that the Universe is all supporting, because we are beings that are derived from the magic of the Source. We exist, just as the greatest, most goodly and most exquisite creation, which is similarly derived from the Sekhem of the Source.

Therefore Hanael draws us to fulfill our soul's purpose, to determine what our life's mission is, how we can shape our destiny clearly and not become lost to chaos. To assist, Hanael also comes forth as the Angel of Courage to help us determine what needs to be done. Through courage, we are drawn to certainty, even in the face of uncertainty, for courage is the virtue that makes us uphold the rightness of a cause when no end is in sight, without promise of reward. Courage is the will to muster on, even if danger, injury, or defeat, appear to be the outcome.

First they ignore you,
then they laugh at you,
then they fight you,
and then you win.

– GANDHI

This is an expression of Hanael's courage. Indeed, those who have proclaimed their truth by returning to the power of love have faced ordeals. At least once, we have all faced confirmed reticence, the ridicule of dismissal, a brandishing ego, the violence of contempt, a rapacious disdain from one who scoffs, an uncaring dismissal from those who are merely committed to a love of power, rather than the power of love. Tests of faith and courage always confirm whom we are as vessels for the Holy Spirit.

THE ORDEALS WE FACE

Ordeals often occur when our role is that of a midwife to a wholly new paradigm, and Hanael helps us with the courage that enlightens our way. This is the courage that beacons our path with the light of the knowledge that, when we think and feel with love, we self-actualize as God. And this is particularly so when we vouch ourselves as co-creators in the ultimate power, to have love in mind forever.

Our minds are made whole by love, for love is holy. Love is always the true purpose of all and, with this in mind, your work will always be oriented to receive joy and abundance. Remember this and your mind will be filled with a power so great that you will feel your soul everlastingly rich in abundance, and your heart and mind will be suffused by an impenetrable power, the power of God's love.

In ancient Egypt, the lioness-headed Goddess Sekhmet was the progenitor of Sekhem, for Sekhmet is the Queen of the Fire, the third eye of the Sun God RA, and the Goddess who creates and destroys. In this, she is closely related to the Shakti of the Hindu pantheon who was responsible for the creation of primordial cosmic energy, and represents the dynamic force that moves throughout the entirety of the Universe, just as was Sekhmet.

Legend has it that one of Sekhmet's quests was to destroy evil armies in Upper Egypt, and yet she developed such blood lust, having slaughtered thousands of warring men, that she literally rampaged, destroying everything and anything in her path. Astonished, the Sun God Ra drew her to reckoning, and stopped the carnage, whilst Thoth placed a spell on her, mollifying, and informing her that there may be another way to cleanse.

This is one of the reasons why Sekhmet henceforth became known to be the protector of the Pharaohs using the fire of her breath, which was also said to have created the natural force of the desert. The holy fire of Sekhmet's breath is the fire breath that wills the power of Sekhem into creation, as an eternal force of creativity. Thus order is restored from chaos.

A DISPROPORTIONATE USE OF FIRE WITHIN SEKHEM

Anger is a force that hardens our heart and distorts the mind. No sense is expressed when anger arises just from outrage, and righteous indignation. However, from an appropriate use of anger, great store may emerge.

We see in the story of Yeshua that, when he entered the Temple of God, and saw it was used by the Money-merchants, he overturned the tables and picked up a whip. The Bible doesn't say he hit anyone, but certainly he gave the whip a good crack, saying: "It is written my house shall be called a House of Prayer, yet you have made it a den of thieves!" Then the blind and the lame came to him and were healed.

This, I feel, is a powerful teaching about anger. Jesus's powerful stance allows us to see the action of saying "No" can be appropriate. But only when the anger isn't arising from the emotions of sheer outrage, or unexpressed superiority – if this is so, we must be cautioned. Ineluctably, love is always the answer and then, like Sekhmet, we calm our passions at the distortions of the world, through the power of alchemy and transmutation, realizing that whatever we see without is also within.

Thoth lulls the outrage of Sekhmet, because he knows his own anger has been transmuted into creativity. He knows he has purified his own sadness at the world's pain. Thoth's use of the magic of Alchemy took anger and transmuted it into compassion, and therefore he was able to cease lamentation about the iniquities of the men, and instead allow his love of humanity to shine forth.

A 'NO' uttered with deep conviction is better than
a 'YES' merely uttered to please, or worse to avoid trouble.

– GANDHI

In the holy moments the clouds of heaven collide in rapturous applause, and mighty thunder is heard, when incidents such as anger occur, the Universe always knows what to do, and when we are hurt, it moves effortlessly to compensate you. If your anger persists, the flow of the Universe distorts and the space/time continuum feels the shock. Whereas, if you release the pain, the hurt is always supplanted by a beautiful miracle and, just like with Jesus, we feel a way of healing those who cannot see or walk easily. We are enabled to show them the path of accuracy, even though our mortal selves may suffer the slings and arrows of outrageous fortune; our divine selves always see the beauty in nature, as Moses did with the burning bush.

Holding on to anger, hurts no one but the angered – the Universe always sees what proportion your hurt amounts to. Then, being a self-correcting cosmic wonder, the Universe immediately makes all things right again. If, however, you further hold onto the hurt, because you feel the cause of what happened was not your responsibility, the miracles are also held onto. On one level, the affect of your wounds shows where the greatest light actually enters, but to hold onto hurt as a form of professional woundology distorts the space-time continuum. It maunders the possibility of feeling better. Then, once we feel our hurt, our despair, our anger, all we need do is honour the fact that it is there by surrendering it to the Holy Spirit and the Angels.

Healing always lies in remembering what is real, and ultimately being without love isn't real. When we remember this, we ascend into the spiritual kingdom where all else drops away, because the reality of Sekhem is immortal. When we are lifted into the immortal worlds, anything that isn't true love simply evaporates, and the world of suffering ceases. Just as Sekhmet was loved by the Sun God RA or RE, for he loved her wrath away, even while she pained through the experience of war.

A CONTEMPORARY PERSPECTIVE

In similar terms, spectacular figures such as Martin Luther King and Mahatma Gandhi must have been outraged by what they saw as moral injustice and spiritual poverty. Yet their practice of 'non-violent peaceful protest' allowed them to be elevated above personal anger into the space of collective emancipation. This spiritual stealth meant that their philosophy would have the possibility of immense longevity. And so long past their assassination, their inheritance lives on, and now motivates groups like the 400 young people on Facebook who began the Egyptian Revolution. What also came to pass as a result of this action informed the US protestors, whose passions were fuelled by the crisis of government: the 'Occupy Wall Street' movement.

Or, as we have seen in late 2013, as the Turkish people of Istanbul, demonstrated against the closure of a major city park, where two hundred year old trees were about to be destroyed, and the area turned into a superfluous shopping mall. The authorities were angered by the protestors, and moved in with the impotent strategy of violence. Yet the protestors, valiant to the core, stood their ground and in some situations offered the soldiers food, acknowledging the nature of human co-creativity and kinship, even though the soldiers aggressively used tear gas.

Non-violence doesn't mean we 'look away' from the horror or conflict. Non-violence means that we 'look through' the carnage with visionary faith, with the zeal and passion of true spiritual sovereignty. This faculty, as we see with Yeshua, means that we become the true miracle worker, and as the healer incarnate with magic, we evoke the world of the immortal in the terrain of the mortal.

Woundology that grips anger means we pledge the aggressor with all our power, and therefore diminish the notion of our own divine self. This behaviour means that we actually give our SEKHEM passion to the darkness of the anger, and not to the shining nature of the light. When we do this, we are doomed to be consumed by loss of power, believing that the one whom we idolatrize is more powerful than God. This way madness lies, and we lose connection with the sustenance that is always provided by the Source.

Thoth's magic creates an alignment within Sekhmet's fiery wrath, and so she is reconnected with the power of her divine-self. This initiation, this transition into ultimate goodness, provides Sekhmet with the truth that penetrates, cutting through all deceit, anger and illusion, to the love-gold within. You see, beyond our anger, beyond our conceit, beyond our pride, lies the gold dust of 'forgiveness' and, when we surrender to this sacred grace, we see the innocence of the guilty party rather than the emotions created by bad temper. Forgiveness liberates, forgiveness is the most powerful emotional sorter – forgiveness takes a full heart to muster its virtuous self.

EVOKING THE WORLD OF THE IMMORTAL

Thoth and Hanael conjure a dream within us, to place forgiveness in each roughshod aspect of our lives, to bring us to a surrender that protects us from any future hurt. If love is thwarted by the breaking of trust, if you were powerfully mistreated and unfairly criticized, if you were insultingly slighted by one whom you thought loved you, if you felt your work or behaviour unjustly dismissed, if the gift of your heart was dashed rudely aside, if the significant other in your life was abusive, if someone cruelly wronged the one you love, and all other slights – all are simply the taskmasters that bring us to account, whereby our life is stripped to the very skin of our being, and exposed for being truly beautiful or awkwardly blemished.

When forgiveness resolves our healing wounds, forgiveness opens the forefront of our consciousness, for forgiveness is a talisman that unlocks the gate to paradise, and loving courage reveals that to love through forgiveness is the only way of truly being real:

> "*I'm sorry,*
> *Please forgive me,*
> *I love you,*
> *Thank you!*"
>
> (– *THE KAHUNA HO'OPONOPONO*)

Through forgiveness, we learn discernment in life and muster the Sekhem force in astonishing ways – for, when a dear one is less than obliging, when we lose patience in traffic, when we lose compassion because someone is rude on the subway, when an adolescent has been outrageous and flagrant in his or her disrespect – if we simply employ forgiveness, we begin to love with an eternal passion.

When you cultivate the passion of Sekhem, you will hold the scars of your physical body as a mark of spiritual endurance, as a badge of wisdom and maturity. Forgiveness is radical, because when we surrender grievance, we also surrender that aspect of our consciousness that holds us back from spiritual correction. If we hold onto the darker forces of martyrdom, anger, hurt or defence, we stifle the natural healing balm of universal splendour, and miracles cease occurring, to the extent that the Sekhem law of attraction abates. Yet, when we honour love, mercy, empathy, kindness and compassion, miracles literally abound.

Self-forgiveness means woundology must be eliminated.

Self-forgiveness means that any behaviour smarting of the 'victim' must cease.

Self-forgiveness means that we see ourselves transparently and authentically.

Self-forgiveness means we are eased of paranoia, delusion and self-recrimination.

Self-forgiveness means we cease blaming and criticizing others.

Self–forgiveness means we release the pain.

Self-forgiveness means we stop reacting through defensiveness.

Self-forgiveness means we substantiate our behaviour through resolution and insight, rather than blame and accusation.

Take a moment right now to discern if you are holding a lack of forgiveness against yourself. If so, bathe in the *Ho'oponopono* and you will feel the difference. This doesn't mean to say that deep hurt doesn't take time, patience and courage to accept fully, to relinquish through forgiveness, through healing. Yet being patient and totally true with forgiveness can utterly change your life, even if it takes these stages of growth. This will eventually allow you to feel the potential free-flowing energy of the source, that is the grace of God's manna feeding you. This is the truth of Sekhem working – in that you will feel yourself soar with the heights of joy, gratitude, surrender, inspiration and love, and the accomplishment.

Robert Browning once wrote: *Ah but a man's reach must exceed his grasp, or what's a heaven for.*

When we reach out for help, God always hears, and the Angels flood to our side, with our Guardian Angel as an intense aid. Then the universe immediately reprogrammes us by sending a miracle, and we rise up refreshed and made new, by the flow of this force, this Sekhem.

HEALING MEANS WHOLENESS

As we heal, the world heals with us. When we stand naked in forgiveness, lightness returns to our hearts and they soar. When we feel this level of reprieve, we know we have made it to a new place, and it might just be paradise. When we feel this degree of Sekhem, our bandwidth expands to absorb more light, becoming as though we were human angels, with a deeper understanding about the centre of our nature and the divinity of our own soul.

THE SEKHEM BLISS OF ATONEMENT

When we falter along the path of life and do not respect Sekhem to stimulate spiritual maturity, we suppress the light by which the pathway to success is illuminated. When we review failure, seeing it simply as the result of an action, we furthermore see failure as a means to learn by.

Any situation that brings us to account by teaching us about wisdom, about humility, about generosity is not a failure, but a courageous lure to being uplifted. When we see those who have achieved success, measuring success as a means to sustained joy, we also know that at some point on their journey they have experienced downfall.

Great achievers are those who have gone deep inside to answer the tyranny of failure with the voice of love. They have dug within to find the power to get back up again. This is done by courage and fortitude, because there is nothing else to do. Spiritually mature people take responsibility for their failures and mistakes, using error as a means to atone, using downfall as a way of developing a thought that heals, whilst using the feeling of forgiveness to wash away any debris accumulated by the wound.

The art of atonement is an amazing default button for our spiritual welfare. When we use this button, the Universe corrects all of our settings concerning the limitations and insecurities. All are reset to programme future grace, and a sigh sounds in the Angelic kingdom.

This is so with all inaccurate thinking and feeling, concerning actions that have been un-loving. When atonement is used, all karma is cleansed. Through an act of contrition past errors are owned, and Sekhem moves us to take full responsibility and make amends.

When atonement is totally conscious, we choose behaviours that are pregnant with forgiveness and self-respect, and so the mercy of the heavens opens to us in seemingly unimaginable ways. For there is no mortal mistake that cannot be divinely corrected.

To err is human, to forgive Divine

– ALEXANDER POPE

As long as we have fully understood the error of our ways, and are choosing to use tender humility to recalibrate our mistakes, then divine mercy fills our hearts and minds, and life shines forth anew from our souls, in order to create the unimaginable.

Within the power of the Divine there is no mistake that cannot be divinely corrected. Mercy is an essential attribute of divine love made human, for mercy is ultimate compassion. When we experience mercy, our breath is momentarily taken from us, for it is from the elixir of prana that mercy emerges. Mercy arrives on Earth like gentle rain directly from Heaven, for mercy is made from the tears of the Angel's love.

Oh think on that,
And mercy then will breathe within your lips
Like man new made.

– *WILLIAM SHAKESPEARE*

Mercy is one of the enchantments of the human experience, and its conviction lies less in the observation than in the dispensation. You see, the Universe will always give us a second opportunity to learn by our mistakes, to not commit them again, and then, when we relinquish the pride that created the error, we begin again to behave like God in his own image, and we release the action of resistance to all that is pure, reaching 'at-one-ment'.

This is when our spiritual compass turns in a new direction towards grace, and we reclaim an inner abundance that eventually, brings outer prosperity, when all is in harmony. This is a promise the holy ones fulfill each time we err, because we are internally programmed to see paradise in all things, thereby reaching our highest creative possibility.

Nothing we can do will stop our soul from the desire of aspiring to be closer to God, for to stand on the shoulders of Giants means we see life only from a divine perspective.

THE SEKHEM BLISS RITUAL MEDITATION

- Find your unique meditation zone for **Silence, Solitude, and Stillness**, whether this be your own sacred space, or a spiritual arbour in nature.
- Check that you won't be disturbed, and consecrate the space by burning incense, lighting a candle, and playing sacred music
- Sit with your spine aligned, keeping your feet on the floor, folding your fingers into a Mudra (thumb and forefinger together), and imagine two vertical channels of gold light vibrating up and down your spine – these replicate the spinal column of Osiris through which Sekhem travels; see them as golden pillars of potential force.
- Imagine the light of these pillars shining down through the base of your spine and penetrating the varying levels of the earth, the soil, the clay, the stone, and the rock – then let the pillars nestle in the

bedrock of Mother Earth.

- Feel the loving charitable force of the Earth being absorbed into the pillars of light, and then once again moving upwards with the love of the divine Mother penetrating through the golden light of the shafts.
- See the light eventually ascending back into your body, filling your heart centre with the love of the Mother, and then on upwards, moving out through the top of your head, and further into the atmosphere of the planet, off to the summit of Father Heaven – that being the Solar Deity of the Universe.
- Once you touch into the Solar Deity see how your whole being is illuminated by the power of the life force of Sekhem, see it as golden light descending down through your body, filling your heart Chakra with glorious light, like a huge Sun burst.
- Then Pause observing the situation, seeing your pranic cord as the two pillars of Osiris's golden light transmitting the force emanated by your connection with the Solar Deity.
- Let all the breath empty from your body, and then breathe in the golden light of RA, the Solar Deity, seeing it move through the column of your spine.
- Breathe wide and deep, allowing the rib cage to swing easily open, as the energy is absorbed into your body. Do this slowly, allowing all the breath to leave your body before you once again breathe in.
- **[Do this gently seven times.]**
- Then chant the OM three times, feeling how the energy resonates through each of your cells – and as we have a hundred trillion cells, be aware of each one resplendent in the light of the Sekhem.
- Pause and again observe the situation.
- Visualize Sekhmet standing close to you protecting your energy field, and truly pleased that you are engaged in this ritual.
- Ask Sekhmet what wisdom she has for you, thanking her for the gift of Sekhem, and then say *RA MA TI MA RA* – which is an ancient Atlantean chant meaning 'everything sacred is blessed': this will sanctify your communication with Sekhmet.
- Reflect on what has just happened and see the force of Sekhem moving through your whole body – through your skin, muscles, ligaments, internal organs, veins and bones.

MICHAEL

COSMIC LEADER

FIVE

THE KA

*It's like you're a fabulously complicated jigsaw puzzle piece, with stunning
colours, oceans of emotion, mountains of possibilities, worlds of talent, and
complex energies. But, as long as you see yourself as just human, you'll never
quite know where you fit in. Please say "No"!'*

– ANGELS OF ATLANTIS

Archangel Michael as the Angel of Endurance overshadows the intelligence of the fifth key with the violet ray of protection and transmutation. Michael knows too well how human desire for longevity – enduring life, withstanding the vicissitudes, recovering from the challenges, wanting to be immune to trauma, wounding or sickness – often misleads. Therefore, Michael reminds us not to believe in the spell of the material world, and to instead see mortal life as a reflection of the immortal, for we made the agreement that our eternal souls would enjoy the human experience – as an aspect of creation, as spirit made flesh.

Michael's use of the violet ray initiates our lives into the ancient art of the Sorcerer's Magic. The Sorcerer functions to be at one with the Source, and to engage with all the elements, of Earth, Water, Air and Fire. In this, the Sorcerer is the Avatar that conjures the elements to alleviate, to abjure, to burn off negativity, to expiate and atone karma, all through the ritual of the Violet Flame.

Michael is positioned thus in our lives, and is the leader of the Angels of Atlantis and, as the leader of our earthly status, Michael endures to help us endure. Michael creates to help us create. Michael shape our soul's destiny, in order to shape the soul that is the Angels pleasure. Michael lasers into our lives, our dominions, into the literal substance of our flesh, to assist with the identification, expiation and atonement of the fate we have wrought.

You see, all self-doubt, all feelings of self-inflicted emotional pollution, all negativity appearing as a major life theme, all physical disease – all can be alleviated by Michael's loving power, because this Archangel uses the integrity of the heart as a number one dialing force, placing truth to lodge deeply within the soul of the human individual.

In this, Michael is often associated with the nature of the Angel of the Reckoning, the weigher of souls – holding in one hand or ray the scales of justice, and in another the sword of truth. Michael is closely associated with the ancient Egyptian ceremony of the weighing of the heart, led by the Goddess Maat, the Conceiver of Truth, and the God Thoth, the great Master Alchemist. Michael has worked closely with Thoth through all Thoth's incarnation, and now is sustained before St Germain, the Ascended Master, in a life that is pledged as the bearer of the Violet Flame.

THE HEART'S TRUTH

In ancient Egypt, the heart was considered as the most precious organ within the body, for the heart was held as a composite of truth, as the seat of the soul. The *Egyptian Book of the Dead* reveals a ritual from those ancient times in which the Jackal-headed God, Anubis, led the dead person before the great scales of justice in the Halls of Truth.

Anubis then placed the heart of the deceased on the left tray of the mighty scales, whilst the feather of Maat, the Goddess of Truth and Justice, was placed on the right tray. If the heart of the deceased outweighed the feather, it meant that the heart was full of darkness from selfish deeds. Conversely, if the heart was lighter than the feather, it was recorded that the deceased had led a righteous life, and could be escorted into Heaven by the King God Osiris, and overshadowed by Thoth, the Holy Scribe of the Gods.

Similarly, Michael draws wisdom from the heart to vanquish the ego, and, for this especial task, for centuries, Michael has been known as the 'Deliverer of the Faithful'. Thus, Michael brings divine creative power to the fore of our lives, cutting through any illusion to create balance, stamina, and reverence in our spiritual odyssey through life. Michael encourages our evolution into personal sovereignty, developing the spiritual integrity that helps us to proclaim the I AM PRESENCE.

The I AM spiritual paradigm is a powerful coda, made known in contemporary times through the bequest of the Ascended Master St Germain. The coda was presented to Guy Ballard on Mount Shasta in the 1930s. Of course, the original teaching came from the root intelligence of Exodus 3:14, when God spoke to Moses through the burning bush, saying: "I AM THAT I AM".

When we join with God's mind thus, when one mind is joined with another in sacred truth, regardless of the position of space or time, that mind can remove whatever binds. So we are delivered to the sweet realm where there is always peace, where all things come full circle, where we are always given a chance to start again in default. Proclaiming one's presence thus means a powerful connection with the sonic radiance of the divine blueprint – *"EHYEH ASHER EHYEH"*.

A PRAYER FOR THE I AM THAT I AM

I AM THAT I AM – EHYEH ASHER EHYEH
Be still, Heart, and tame My Mind
I AM a divine instrument of the I AM
I AM the flow of the Cosmos
I AM the breath of life
I AM the unconditional love flame that shimmers for all life
I AM in supplication to the Divine Mother Earth
I AM in supplication to the Divine Father Heaven
I AM in service to all that is humble, innocent and true
Mighty I AM presence, please consume my doubts, fear and judgment,
    and allow me to be a pillar of courage
I AM in this holy instant surrendering my heart
I AM the force of love and generosity
I AM the dazzling experience of embodiment
I AM as human a living form of your Divinity
I AM the shimmering light of the Holy Spirit
I AM the fire of Heaven
I AM the mighty presence in action
Be strong, My Heart, and sing the Song of My Soul

–THE ANGELS OF ATLANTIS

Traditionally, throughout Christian, Hebrew, and Islamic scholarship, Michael was ascribed the role of 'holding the keys to the kingdom of heaven'. Furthermore, in Muslim lore, Michael is assigned an innumerable array of Angels, who on his behalf implore the pardon of Allah in order to expiate the negativity of willful people. In this chapter, Michael brings us information about this electrical key to paradise known as the KA.

THE ETHERIC SHEATH MECHANISM

The KA is the unique soul power that individualizes within our Etheric sheath. Thus, the KA creates from light an exact replica of the physical body, holding the original soul template in holographic form. The Etheric sheath is the first sheath of electro-magnetic energy around the body, and is the archetype from which the physical form is built. All life forms have Etheric sheaths, whether they be Solar, Planetary, or Devic as in the kingdom of the nature spirits.

The Etheric sheath overshadows the physical body and conditions its bio-culture by storing up the radiance of the solar power from the Sun, and transmitting light through the Chakras. Therefore, the Etheric body consists of a multitude of finely laced nerve channels, or *nadis,* that form a boundary between the physical and astral plane, creating a powerful network of transmitting fibres that literally forms a generating battery. This in turn empowers the physical body, radiating throughout the whole aura.

Further to this, the constituent parts of your Light field are the:

Physical body
Etheric sheath
Astral plane
Mental essence
Soul or Causal emanation
Buddhic/Christic presence
Atmic consciousness

In order to fully understand these seven aspects of the I AM potential, let me briefly explain:

Physical – the body that you are all too familiar with.

Etheric – this is the elemental light body of the KA that we are exploring in this chapter.

Astral – this is the light body of your star-seed presence, connecting with your emotional field, and is refined by the experience of transmuting desire through the higher self, so that the conscious mind governs the emotional body.

Mental – this is the essence body of your thoughts, which lives through your consciousness creating reality, and therefore steers your life through consistent specificity and perseverance.

Soul or **Causal** – this is the soul body that exists on a higher mental plane, which fuels the intuitive, abstract mind, and records each aspect of your karma.

Buddhic – this is the plane of light that associates your soul with the higher essence of your soul's counsel, linking you with the Buddha and the

Christos energies.

Atmic – this is the plane of existence which appears as the vehicle of identification for being at one with the I AM PRESENCE, which is the aspect of the Light field that moves us to attain self-mastery – the beginning of our trajectory towards Ascended Master status.

As we evolve through countless lives in search and yearning for ascension, our full light body awakens, and so we again merge with our Monad, our Soul Group, which is the launching point for our eternal and infinite self. This kingdom lies beyond the transition we normally refer to as 'death', for in truth there is only 'mere' completion, before we meet the trajectory that takes us back into eternity.

THE GRACE OF COSMIC EXISTENCE

Archangel Michael teaches that the key to paradise known as the KA fully activates as we release the indentation of karma from our energy field, as we heal the thought and feeling pollutions that corrupt our being, as we truly become one in faith with our divine origins. Because, you see, there is a kingdom that we are from which awaits us. This is a realm of infinite creative potential that exists beyond the mortal mind, and within the mind of God.

The mind of God is the spiritual essence of the Universe, and when we choose to totally believe in this Mind, we become liberated by the grace of cosmic existence.

Our cosmology draws us through the rite of countless initiations, and therefore the spiritual devotee aligns incongruence with the higher levels of reality. The Universe is programmed to manifest through you and your life in a multiplicity of ways. The Universe seeks out creativity through you. The Universe wants you to find the highest possible joy. The Universe intends for you to expand your material existence, not by just acquiring more material possessions, but by living a life of sustainable love and joy, until your life becomes filled with the ultimate ecstasy of the ever-cascading **Light**.

This light drenches us whilst cascading through and from the Eighth Chakra. That occurs when we have purified the lower Chakras and are embracing the full impulse of the Universal Heart. This Chakra brings oneness through unity-consciousness. Thus, the spiritual initiate pours light like a fountain from the Eighth Chakra, light which is the halo or aura we see around the Shining Ones – as for example in Renaissance Art.

The lighter we become, the more we elevate onto higher octaves, with the Angels literally carrying us to even newer heights. The Angels vibrate in service to the creative consciousness of cosmology, and it is within the form of this cosmology, that God's mind expressly accommodates us. God's mind never refers to us as being too old, too inadequate, too inexperienced, or too much of a failure. In God's mind, there are no mistakes that we aren't given an opportunity to correct. Within God's mind, there is no substance or behaviour that cannot be compensated for.

Thinking thus opens us to our Divine Ka, and the emissions of our light body radiate a sacred connection with the crystalline grid of the planet, which is the web of energy that is the Gaia's personal matrix of light. Indeed, Divine KA is a flowing emanation of the God Source, both Mother and Father God, which connects us with the crystalline grid of the Universe, the love light circuitry.

When thus connected, our light is literally switched on by our KA, and becomes a bio-plasmic field of vast potential. This is the force from which we derive the ability to be a catalyst. This is where our facility to manifest bounty and abundance emanates from. This is the field from which our bodies create miracles. This is the force from which we connect with the supreme intelligence of the cosmos.

As we turn these pages of cosmic wisdom, our lives feel destined to create unique events, our souls appear as bridges between the worlds of thought and feeling, of Heaven and of Earth, and opportunities abound for the expansion of our creativity in service to the planet.

To live one's life as though it were a thought made by God is to live miraculously. To live the joy of the Angels is to expand the mind of God. To live by love is to gain dominion over the lower thought-forms of the world. To live through hope is to see messages of love written upon the sky. To live in faith is to feel that love exists purely to bring joyful credence to God. To live in charity is to see the Angels and Ministers of Grace spreading their light through the life of planet Earth: The life that is currently teeming with Angelic transmissions, ET sightings, Elemental Spirits, Crop Circle manifestations, and palpable information about paranormal activity, in the form of Ghosts and Spirit, etc.

THE ANGELIC COMMUNION

Your Divine KA is aligned with the Angelic communion, because your KA is plugged into the energy field from which Angels and Ministers of Grace arise. Angels are Angels, and exist as primordial light forms, as orb-like plasma beings that arise from the thoughts of God. These orb wanderers come to pledge loving assistance to us, to remind us that our hearts are the seat of our soul, so that we may transform the disguise that many of us have worn for centuries over our hearts, in denial of our souls.

For we Human Angels were seeded in the mists of time, from star-seeds we arise, to act as Guardians for those that have forgotten whom they truly are. Thence we are coded to awaken the true nature of every human being here on Earth; to enliven the presence of soul in physical form, and through the currency of feeling, for feeling is the language of the soul.

Angels live to feel, whereas human beings live to know. Angels do not need schooling as humans do, for they know the essence of everything through their highly electrified intuition. Intuition is the soul of great thinking. Intuition is the super highway that carries the Angel's distinct magic. Intuition sounds like the laughter of a bubbling brook, or the gurgling of a babe, or the wind moving through the trees, or the inspiration of lovers sweetly loving.

The Angels' love is inspirational, for they live within the hosting vibration of divine will and, as such, their knowledge is the vibration of the heart. Knowing, loving, praising and prophecy are the slipstream expressions of these exquisite orb beings and, in this, they teach us about the evolutionary forces within the cosmos, a holy cup filled with an elixir from which we may drink eternally.

When this force quenches our thirst, it enlivens our KA, and we fully activate our sacred communion with the planet. Planet Earth is a vehicle of life in the evolution of the Cosmos. It is set for a specific course, and as we are mindful of this, we live each moment to draw the Christ consciousness onto the planet, and into our bodies. Thus, we encourage a vast inter-dimensional shift to take place, and the mask that was once placed over our soul's intelligence millennia ago is removed. Thus, the suit of the old patriarchal disguise literally melts from our bodies.

Then we awaken the Divine KA and our potential is vast, and so it is prophesied. In the foreseeable future, we as intelligent planetary life forms possess the inherent ability to evolve a triple helix DNA, eventually developing twelve strands of DNA. As we evolve to this level of light fusion, we begin to live an advanced spiritual intelligence, formed by the combination of all seven Chakras melding with the first trans-personal Chakra – the Eighth – and then into the further four Chakras. This creates a portal of unity, through which we recalibrate universal heart consciousness, and so we fuse with the Christos, and become human Angels.

Social surveys suggest that nine out of ten people living in the United Kingdom believe in Angels, and two thirds of the population of the United

States of America do so as well. Our belief in these supernatural beings means that we are becoming more mature in regard to our spirituality, and so our intuitions reflect this. Then the trajectory of our spiritual maturity accelerates, our sensitivity expands, and the KA body becomes more highly attuned.

THE CHALLENGE OF THE KA

The postscripts of the European Industrial Revolution, advanced Education and the rise in literacy, have brought great advances in technology, and yet have also negated much of our extra-sensory awareness. This is particularly so with regard to the KA's intuitive sensing, psychic acuity, the power of finer feeling, and the sensibility that embraces harmony.

Through harmony and coherence human nature seeks the path of least resistance, seeking liberation, honourably searching for the innate spirituality, desiring to know the origin and purpose of all things. And so we move, at this remarkable time of portal opening, to reveal our intuitive mind as a sacred gift. We become alerted to the Angelic Realms, the Devic Kingdoms, and the feats of human endurance, which bring about miracles and convey great magic about the soul.

During the maturing patterns of your KA, as your intuition soars, it is highly likely that you will encounter the Orb Wanderers, whether they be Angels or Devic Spirits, because your vibration will rise to a higher frequency, enhancing your intuitive powers. This largely occurs because the Angel's light-filled body affects vast change within your own light body, downloading into your physique, into your Chakra system, and allowing you to feel extra-sensory processes taking place. If you are concerned, say a prayer of love and light, and you will feel automatically comforted by the Angel's benediction.

Here is a prayer for Michael that exemplifies these points:

A PRAYER TO ARCHANGEL MICHAEL

> *Dear Archangel Michael,*
> *Please fill me from the brow to the toe with your celestial Violet Light, allowing me to see my soul's core, to witness the beauty of my KA, and to shape its destiny from this force.*
> *Please give me the skill of my oracular knowledge so that I might take full charge of my spiritual evolution, and be the sovereign of my own frequency as a life unfolding of the Universe.*
> *Please purify my attention to see the constant glowing violet flame*

of the Source, of the Divine Light within me, so that I am always honed by unconditional love.

Please protect me in peace, so that my mind and body are the healthy life I wish to be.

I send love and joy.

And so it is.

Amen.

MANIFESTING YOUR INTUITION
AS EXTRA SENSORY PERCEPTION

- You will experience the need to honour your physical presence by eating food and fluid filled with light, and so regulating your light fusion through breathing exercises and other restoratives such as Acupuncture or Osteopathy. This physical attention to detail will promote the evolution of your empathic clairvoyance – seeing psychic or spiritual energy through light, colour and imagery. You see, the shining ones download their communications to us through finer sensing in our bodies, and therefore the KA receives the radiation, increasing activity within the pineal and hypothalamus, and producing psychic phenomenon.

- You will experience the growing awareness of clairaudience and clairsentience through hearing or sensing psychic energy. This may come in the form of high-pitched sounds, or literal voice manifestation. So often voices are heard as one's higher self. Perhaps unusual smells may also emanate from the ether.

- You will receive oracular information from higher levels of consciousness, particularly from beings in the fifth to seventh dimension, such as your Guardian Angel and Spirit Guides.

- You will find it necessary to join other kindred spirits, who will provide support and grounded balance. Also, spiritual counseling may be in order to help you manage and coordinate the new energies coming through your KA.

- You will feel it necessary to release all emotional disturbance from your life,and, having cleansed the immediate rapport you have with emotional ties, you will feel the power of remote viewing developing, for, when we cure our feeling body, we accelerate our soul's maturing and the KA shines.

- You may experience downloading information from the Akashic Records.

- You will be led to comprehend past lives that have a specific conviction for you as you unravel your KA's intelligence.

The facility to feel freely – the possibility to participate in a life filled with joy – allows the KA to vibrate at an extremely accelerated rate. Positivity is much more than the literal absence of the negative, positivity mobilizes; it is the literal presence of the positive that draws our hearts to sacred ecstasy. A powerfully compassionate teacher of mine is HH the Dalai Lama who said: *Happiness is a decision, not a condition!*

Thinking loving thoughts has a miraculous power. When we think of someone we love, we feel the soul contract we have entered into with them, and in this I mean, those we have true contact with, not the fantasies! When we make soul contact with someone, we engage with their highest good, and therefore bring about expression of their higher self. This creates synergy, and so we are met on a level that increases our own highest self – this inevitably brings an opportunity of optimized creativity, filled with the breath of the Holy Spirit.

Whatever brings people together creates energetic contracts, and when we meet kindred souls, we realize that we are meeting on a wholly different spiritual trajectory that brings a higher reckoning, for they bring a unique sense to bear. Then we see how our souls have met, sometime, somewhere else. You see, core relationships are divinely crafted, and are destined to heal the world. They are brought together by the intelligence of the Universe for one purpose: for the enlightenment of all concerned.

A MEDITATION TO KA GAZE AND LIGHT CLEANSE

- Make sure you have **Silence, Solitude and Stillness**.
- Move to your enchanted sacred space, whether this be in nature or in your own beautiful home.
- Dim lights, burn incense, play muted sacred music that elevates the vibration you wish to create, all of which consecrates the space with a divine countenance.
- Make sure you switch off information technology.
- Find somewhere to sit with an aligned spine – feel the weight of your body with your feet earthed, and your back long.
- Breathe out your force and relax, then breathe in the healing light of the Universe… feeling the Holy Prana as a brightly coloured silver light moving through the whole of your body relaxing you, creating stillness, healing anything that isn't integrated… do this

three times, letting your body sink deeper and deeper into ease.

- Visualize your KA as your 'double' – sitting opposite you – see the KA as utterly transparent and crystalline.

- Observe your KA, see its dimension. You may view it pulse or shift the currents of your field – ask what it is showing you about your sacred connection with the Source.

- Look with an attention that goes deeper and deeper into the presence of your KA, and you will see not just the outline of your light field – the aura – but also the manifestation of your power centres, or Chakras.

- Where do you locate the power most in your body? Which Chakras are spinning easily, and which are held? This you can deduce by determining your life's path through your body. For example, are you muscularly healthy and aware of your being's form, or are you un-centered? Are you a great communicator, or do you process information by holding it in your body, making your kinesthesia dull or overweight? Where do you hold yourself back from expression? Where do the tensions sit in your body? Are you head-centered, or body-centered?

- All these questions, and others like them, will encourage you to look deeply into the light of your KA, to see if there are any tears in your field. These torn light-energies will show as coloured lines, or spaces of darkness, maybe even different colours or tones from the silver light we visualized earlier.

- What you will see will either feel free-flowing, or will appear blocked.

- Firstly, breathe widely and deeply three times, and you will notice your KA brighten, become larger, and shimmer with the light of Pranayama.

- Allow the breath, as a silver light, to circulate through the whole of your physical body, through all of your organs, and notice the powerful influence this has on your KA.

- If you feel as though you have an injurious connection with a person or a place, you will see this reflected in your KA… therefore decide to sever your connection with that person or place.

- If you feel there is something that needs healing in your body, then allow the light of the Universe to spread through the area that needs healing.

- Observe the crystalline nature of your KA and see where there may be discolorations, and go deeper into this mirror of your life.

- As you look, see if you have lines of force like tendrils of energy emerging from your KA – if present you will probably see them arising from certain Chakras and, if you can see these, they will be drawn to the person or place you have the negative connectivity with. Determine what is the emotional holding that you appear to have with that person or place.

- Place your hands over your heart, left over right, and breathe in widely and deeply generating fire in your heart and thence into your KA, then cut the cords on an out-breath, with a laser light created by your force severing the tie.

- Then breathe Holy Prana deeply at least three times into your Heart Centre, building your power, seeing how your KA's energy is replenished with the much purer energy.

- If the light cords are stubborn and do not sever through thought, raise your hands above your head, and through action bring your hands down like a sword, whilst you say: "*I am secure, I am healed, **all is well**, and I'm a perfect match for my core vibration*".

- Repeat this until you feel the light cords fully released or severed, then cross your right hand over your left hand placing them on your heart centre – breathe in the feeling of liberation, and taking an even wider, deeper breath chant *KA… KA… KA* on three separate energies, then see your KA glistening with your reunited force, cleansed, exorcised and surging through the power of this cleanse.

- Then turn the chant to the most sacred syllable, three times sounding the *primo mobile OM… OM… OM…* which will sanctify your whole presence.

- Pause, be aware of your Guardian Angel's presence, and notice that you are surrounded not just by the light of this Angel but also by Archangel Michael's Orb Presence. Michael appears as the Angel of Endurance to help you, bringing you the courage to heal the reason for which you drew the negativity to you in the first place.

- The call of *KA* is the sonic key that will always brings Archangel Michael to your side, and so feel Michael's presence as an all enveloping Violet Mist.

- Archangel Michael is the champion of the **Violet Flame**, and so feel the Violet Mist moving deeply within your whole being, helping you to transmute the energy of the past.

- Once you are completed with the process, view your KA surrounded in a Violet Aura, protecting the sensitive nature of what you have created; deeply reflect on the nature of what has happened.

- Spend at least twenty minutes recovering from the intensity of what you have just accomplished, and drink water.

REASONS FOR THE KA MALFUNCTIONING

- Trauma
- Denial of the heart's intelligence
- Past life corruption
- Distortions within the soul's spiritual lineage
- Ancestral & personal karma
- Physical disability or sexual/creativity challenges
- Crystalline distortions within the cellular structure
- Psychic attack
- Denial of one' soul path
- Unresolved anger issues
- Controlling behaviour
- Toxic disturbance from drugs or environment

If you feel that any of these possibilities occur within your KA, then please seek out either a medical practitioner for the physical challenges, or a complementary specialist when the issue is metaphysical.

THE HEART GENERATES KA

The physical organ that claims our love and governs our physical constitution is the Heart. The metaphysical heart is also a gateway to unification, linking us with higher intelligence, drawing together into coherence both thinking and feeling. The heart opens us to the kingdom of the intuition – the domain of the imagination – where the divine and the mundane meet in an ecstasy of finer feeling.

Now here is my secret, a very simple secret; it is only within the heart that one sees rightly; what is essential is invisible to the naked eye.

SAINT-EXUPÉRY

The heart is not a sentimental organ. It is forthright, brave and substantial, supporting and nourishing our body systems during a lifelong commitment to excellence. The heart generates huge power for the KA – stimulated by the insights and awareness we bring to consciousness, through the countless initiations of life – '*the thousand natural shocks that flesh is heir to*' – and so we mature into our personal power, reaching a place of coherent centeredness that offers nobler and higher choices.

This is particularly rich when we engage in physical and emotional experiences that produce 'heart coherence' and a literal heart expansion such as these 'Heart Tingle' processes:

Love
Delight
Compassion
Joy
Non-judgment
Pleasure
Patience
Devotion
Forgiveness
Jubilance
Thrill
Adventure

The Heart Math organization has recently conducted studies that discovered the average human being thinks 60,000 thoughts a day, and 50,000 of those thoughts are negative.

If we engage in 'Heart Stabs', our energy field depletes, our heart shrinks, and our KA automatically diminishes. We then engage in feeling states such as:

Worry
Sadness
Frustration
Guilt
Hurt
Hatred
Anger
Depression
Loathing
Fear
Terror
Grief

The heart has a seismic power both within the life to which it is dedicated, and within the life of the planet on which it resides. It is well documented that the human heart generates an electro-magnetic field far stronger than any other organ within the body, the power of which is 5,000 times greater than the human brain.

MEDITATION FOR SOUNDING YOUR KA

- Make sure you have **Silence, Solitude and Stillness.**
- Prepare the way for your unique KA sounding, by entering your sacred space and closing the door.
- Consecrate the space by burning incense, lighting candles, and saying a prayer to Archangel Michael such as:

Dear Archangel Michael,
Please bring your love & joy to this place, purifying my sanctuary, and allowing it to be a place of ultimate heart coherence.
I give this time of purifying my KA to you, that it may be a time of rich quietude.
Please dissolve my thoughts of stress and fear, and deliver me to that space where all is well, where all is in alignment with the Divine plan.
Amen

- Sit with your spine aligned, feeling your weight, and assume the mudra by bringing your thumb and finger together – which connects the powerful current of the sun and moon connected within your body.
- Empty all your breath through your lips, wait for a moment feeling the need to breathe, then breathe in, and as you feel the Prana filling your being, see the energy of Michael's Violet Ray, within the breath force, filling your inner space. Allow the energy to move down the whole of your spine, illuminating your Djed, rather like an elevator moving down through your spine. Then sigh out.
- Repeat the breathing process seven times, changing each mudra to a different finger each time you breathe, until you have touched each finger tip with your thumb (and the breath) and then bring all your fingers together for the remaining breaths, and *HUM* through your heart each time, on each of the seven breaths to the point of their conviction.

- This will fuel the fire of your KA and allow Archangel Michael to pour Angelic Elixir into your being. The Angels always arise from the essence of love, and so be with this intention as you breathe in and then out on the *HUM*.

- Pause and notice the delicious stillness that wraps your energy field, allowing your KA to shimmer. You may even hear ringing in your ears, as you feel the gracious presence of Michael surrounding you, overshadowing the purification of your KA, and allowing it to be filled with the Angelic presence of this great Cosmic Leader.

- Now tune into another breath, and this time take it deep into your body, into your Pelvic area and sound *EL…* for as long as the breath will sustain itself.

- Whilst chanting this mantra for the Earth have in mind the trust of Archangel Uriel as a beautifully rich Quartz Pink orb, and know Uriel to be responsible for the **Earth** element in your life. You can chant this three times if you wish.

- Then move to the Solar Plexus and chant *EEM* through a sustained breath, enchanting the **Water** element into your being, which is overshadowed by the grace of the Blue Orb of Archangel Gabriel – again, chant this three times if you wish.

- Then chant *OM* in your Throat Chakra, which evokes the **Air** element governed by the beautiful Green Orb of Archangel Raphael.

- Then chant again *KA* drawing the Violet Orb of Archangel Michael even deeper into your KA force initially through the Crown Chakra of your head.

- This chant is other-worldly and is given by the great Archangels of Atlantis, and so you will feel a powerful shift in your consciousness, activating force in your whole being.

- Be still for a moment and notice how the energies dance around you, shimmering within your KA… feel yourself utterly protected by Michael's powerful Violet presence, cascading waves of energy throughout your field.

- When using *EL EEM OM KA* one often sees a spiraling light moving through their whole being rather like the ascending and descending light of the Djed, or double helix DNA system in our bodies.

- The Chant alters our genetic force and may appear as a rainbow.

- On using this Mantra you will feel your force encouraging your KA to shimmer fully.
- Record the sensations, and reflect accordingly.

ZADKIEL

DIVINE COMFORTER

SIX

✝HE AB

*The secret chamber of your heart is like a Crystal Cave where a great Magician
resides. In silence the Magician gifts you a connection to the most precious of
cosmic forces, the portal presence of universal co-creativity. The energy centre
of your Heart Chakra will allow you to partake of a quintessential remembering, will allow you to utterly sense whom you truly are, as a quanta of light:
human and yet suffused with the membrane of all that is divine.*

– THE HEART SPEAKS

The force of AB is centered within the heart and, according to the time
honoured customs and traditions of ancient Egypt, is known as the foundation of all life, comprising of the very seat of the soul.

Each beat of the heart pulses a holy instant through the spiraling energy
of the heart's soft tissue, and so the powerful symbol of infinity is formed,
part prophecy, part longevity, part eternal providence, for the content of
the AB energy in the heart is timeless.

Within the human heart, the symbol of infinity forms a metaphoric
crystal chamber, whose walls reverberate with the eternal jewels of love,
empathy, compassion, joy, courage, patience, forgiveness, gratitude and
peace. These gems are ancient in their stored wisdom, stirring the presence and character of infinity, allowing the precious cargo of the heart to
permeate the whole of your being, radiating through each gesture and each
behaviour.

Thus, by the presence of this treasure, we make manifest the will of
God. For God's will is the magical light that shines through all beings,
all kingdoms, and all elements. God's will loves 'creation' into existence,
bringing Divine order into manifestation, in this case within human form.

The AB force manifests through the light of the heart, created by the
impulse of unconditional love, and enjoined with the spirit of the Cosmos.
When we evoke the precious jewels of the heart, we co-create intelligent
new paradigms with astonishing authenticity, steered not by us but by
God's love. When our hearts are called to love like this, we become hosts
to God and, when we yield to this quality of loving, we optimize our pur-

pose and unfolding. Each aspect points in the one direction, to focus us in balance and peace. This free breath, this pure pulse, this cosmic flow, this restored balance bring absolute love to the sanctity of each moment.

THE ANGEL OF DIVINE COMFORT

To hallow this act, the Archangel Zadkiel protects and overshadows the AB, for Zadkiel is the Divine Comforter, and commissioned thus throughout the stories of yore. This is the Archangel who helped Adam forgive when he was removed from the Garden of Eden, after the dramatic transition from innocence to experience. This is the Archangel who stayed the hand of Abraham from slaughtering his son Isaac. This is the Archangel who protected Lot from becoming a pillar of salt at the fall of Sodom. For these acts, we see Zadkiel as an agency by which the supreme vibration of gratitude is given and received, and so our own thanks see's Zadkiel stand in heaven alongside Gabriel, as one of the Shinanin – 'the glory holders' of God.

This glorious Angel electrifies our presence with the multi-faceted vibrations of the benevolent heart. We feel these vibrations as 'heart tingles' when we warm to the love, empathy, delight, peace and compassion that arise directly from the Source. Indeed, the protection and comfort of Zadkiel fortifies our lives with a wealth of knowledge concerning the vulnerability and fragility of our own process, for that is intrinsically what we are, as we vibrate with feeling, the language of the soul.

Refined feelings like love and empathy are vulnerable to touch, and so Zadkiel shields us from the demons, distortions, projections and fears that come along as we journey through life. Zadkiel teaches us that we alone can overcome the anguish by drawing the purity of our soul to triumph over the darkness. It is through the maxims that *thought creates reality*, and *feeling actualizes manifestation,* that we wake to the freedom of knowledge. Then we realize that there is nothing on Earth that's good or bad – it is thinking that makes it so. So our first choice is happiness, and then heaven unfolds right in front of our eyes.

When we begin to vibrate with this quality of force, Zadkiel steps forth, bestowing wisdom upon us, allowing us a clearer vision of any obstacle that creates the self-limiting patterns that hold us back. These patterns are the impediments that stop us from touching our own abundant joy and power, so Zadkiel lovingly shows us what needs to be brought forth into the light of the AB and then healed.

Then, when fully identified and transmuted, Zadkiel aids us again to open our hearts so that divine grace may pour in. Then we can aspire to joy, feeling love, generosity and kindness pervading through our entire world, so we unearth what on earth we are on Earth to be!

Working with Zadkiel means a continuous flow of abundant treasure, as this supreme Archangel knows how to dispense divine love, orientating our spiritual compass, and all created by an intense, immense, and intimate love for the human soul. In these aspects, Zadkiel draws unconditional love directly from the Universe, for Zadkiel teaches us that there is no scarcity within the Source. Rather, that it is a dominion of infinitely unfolding creative possibility, full of love and joy. It is only we who budget these God-given energies, believing that there will never be enough, rather than believing in the splendour of creative abundance.

In this, Zadkiel teaches us sublimely, reigning supreme over the province that reveals utter benevolence, mercy and grace, teaching us to trust in God's will as the excellence of the Universe because, if anything falls from divine order, it is immediately self-corrected by universal force. *All we need do is to let go and let God in.* All we need be is to trust the bounty of the Universe. All we need is for Source energy to become so clear to us, all we need is to allow Heaven to open its gates, and there, in the unseen nature of the bliss, everything is spotlessly clean, all gadgets work, dust never settles, and all human beings are as fit as a fiddle.

THE SEISMIC POWER OF THE AB

Zadkiel reminds us that the heart, as the AB, has a seismic power both in the life to which it is dedicated, and for the life of the planet on which it resides. It is well documented that the human heart generates an electro-magnetic field that has been scientifically measured as moving beyond two or three meters around the body. This encourages the vibration of AB, and expands the muscle and flesh of the heart. This potential is vast for, if this could be created by the 7.5 billion people residing on the Earth, it would measure miles or metres beyond the girth of our planetary home.

The heart resonates through its own magnetic field, pulsing to the rhythms of how we feel. Each emotional sway, each feeling quake, each response that moves us affects our internal organs and watery landscape. This occurs through the balance or imbalance of our hormones, the flow of blood, water and plasma, the rhythm of cellular regeneration, the expression of our physical force. Each emotional tide responds to the heart, and communicates with our outer field – indeed, with the entire outer locale of our lives.

When our AB energy forms a core life balance, our emotions live positively, promoting an acceleration of biological activity that stimulates harmony via the production of serotonin and oxytocin. Conversely when negative emotions abound, other bio-chemical changes rapidly occur producing the stress hormones of adrenaline and cortisol, bringing chaos to the organ of the Heart, including muscular aches, mental confusion, a lack of equilibrium, and negative emotional states that super-charge our intimate relationships with deleterious effects.

Seeing life through this perspective allows us to make the mature choice of creating a new and more exciting potential. If we can effectively learn the language of the heart, if we can open to love unconditionally, we alter the earth's magnetic field. So we alter the effect the field has over all planetary life, meaning that the animal, vegetable, and mineral kingdoms will totally change, creating the boundless effect of a new worldview.

This is the work of all the Archangels like Zadkiel who, as emissaries of the light, turn our hearts and minds to fully use the keys to paradise.

THE KEY TO THE AB OF THE HEART

In September 2001, two geostationary environmental satellites, positioned in orbit 22,300 miles (35,880 km) over the equator detected a huge shift in the globe's magnetic field, and this forever altered the view of the scientific establishment. These powerful shifts occurred fifteen minutes after the first plane hit the World Trade Center on September 11th, and then again fifteen minutes before the second plane hit.

Studies conducted at Princeton University in the USA, and in allegiance with the non-profit organization HeartMath – which exists to teach core Heart tools for emotional intelligence – found that the correlation between the magnetic shifts on 9/11, and the events themselves were more than a coincidence. Indeed, the satellites had registered something similar happening during the tragic events of August 21st 1997, when Diana, Princess of Wales, died.

Both events indicate clearly that the emotional intention of individual and collective AB forces, arising from the hearts of billions of people, vastly affects the Globe's magnetic field, and so heaven alone knows what happened on April 29th, 2011 when 4,500,000,000,000,000 – that's four and a half billion people around the world viewed via TV or Internet screening processes the marriage of Prince William and Kate Middleton. This effectively means that more than half the world's population watched two young people beautifully and elegantly plight their love troth, on a day that will go down in the annals of history.

With this in mind, Archangel Zadkiel inspires a brilliant plan: If the magnetic field is stimulated by feeling states that also produce war or peace, economic scarcity or abundance, societal loss or gain, climate tragedy or balance, then humanity has at its disposal a fascinating neo-paradigm, a leading-edge frontier for human evolution to literally change negativity for ever.

A NEW WORLD VIEW: ENLIGHTENMENT

Evolutionary aspects of our mortal lives, created through prayer, bring us to know other aspects of our soul's immortal life. Prayer is a means by which we talk to the Divine, and meditation is when we listen.

The essence of prayer evokes change via a power much greater than anything our own will can achieve. By placing precise and conscious thought through the vector of unconditional love, directly towards heaven, we literally accomplish the miraculous. Indeed, *A Course in Miracles* teaches that: *Prayer is the medium of miracles, when the Creator directly communicates with the Created.*

Living thus means we shift from ego-based thought into spirit-based thinking, and so plug back into the eternal power of the Source. There, the electricity of love-joy lights us up and, infused thus, we flow through the creativity of the ALL THAT IS, which has existed forever and aye.

Can we truly choose a thought that illuminates and activates the love-light circuitry throughout the whole of our lives? This is crucial because deactivating our connection from the Source means that we become fixated by the material world, rather than living life through the exquisite power of love. Living life through love requires bravery and courage and, when living thus, Archangels like Zadkiel help us move the force of our AB, via the conduits of prayer and meditation, to achieve spiritual and social revolution.

Intellectualizing about our position doesn't carry sufficient sway to bring about radical change. What we need is a new way of being, in order to recalibrate our journey from the head to the heart, and the Angels intimate that this way of being – connecting with our hearts and linking with the knowledge that we are not alone, but all one – wholly changes our worldview.

The Angels are currently here through a great wave of Angelology, possibly the third great wave since creation itself 13.7 billion years ago. They know all too well that we need powerful spiritual assistance in order to make the transitions that are necessary, to create this trajectory that will allow us to alter the strategies that create the woeful nature of our world

– that two billion people live on less than two US Dollars a day, that five thousand children die each day through hunger-related causes or disease, that one billion people at this moment are severely malnourished, that three thousand people die every day through suicide, and much, much more. The Angels wish to powerfully help us create a better world.

Einstein suggested that the world's problems would not be transformed by the same level of thinking used to create them, instead what must occur is a wholly new strategy, a wholly different worldview, and one based on holistic principles that arise from different brain waves.

The intuitive mind is a sacred gift and the rational mind is a faithful servant. We have created a society that honors the servant and has forgotten the gift.

– EINSTEIN

Enlightenment may appear at first to be abstract, until it is literally taken from the head to the heart. For we've all experienced the force that sparkles with the courage of human will, or the passionate speech that amounts to something much more than mere intellectualization. We must desist from perpetuating ideas solely in our heads, by literally bringing them to our bodies as experiences. We've all met people who indicate through their vociferous opinions what books they have read, and yet appear to have no real experience of what they read, or how to embody the intelligence they've described.

Those who know others are wise,
Those who know themselves are enlightened.

– LEONARDO DA VINCI

Firstly, we need to understand that a major change from our normal way of thinking must occur. Normalcy means we mostly use Beta Brain Waves throughout our daily consciousness. This arises from the purely mechanistic way we live our lives, whereas our hearts yearn for a deeper part of our consciousness to be accessed, which can occur through Alpha and Theta Waves. When these are achieved, we elicit the power of transformative consciousness, and when this is drawn forth into our everyday lives, our psyche evolves as our brains change gear. When this is experienced within our living process, we find a key that opens a level of consciousness where great magic lies.

Alpha waves open a bridge between our rational and intuitive mind.

They calm us from the frenzy of 'doing, doing, doing', and allow us to access that still small voice of calm, which produces expansive cellular regeneration, promoting health and inner peace.

Theta waves open us to the unconscious mind, that deep subterranean meditative realm where the soul lives, and where we experience an absolute knowing that God is real, for here we connect with the cosmic principle of the ALL THAT IS.

Meditation is a much richer practice than one that simply reduces stress. Meditation provides us with a gateway to a much deeper understanding of soul, where fissures of consciousness open to profound insight, inspired action, holistic understanding, amplified perspective, expanded conviction, and deep love or peace. From love and peace arises a greater unfolding of the human spirit, which the rational mind alone cannot achieve.

> *If the doors of our perception were cleansed every thing would appear,*
> *as it is, Infinite. For man has closed himself up,*
> *till he sees all things through the narrow chinks of his cavern.*
>
> – *WILLIAM BLAKE (18TH CENTURY MYSTIC)*

Enlightenment occurs when we embody the experience of the miraculous caress of the 'infinite'. For the experience of knowing is a sensation, not a thought. When we align rational thought with soulful feeling, we recalibrate our psyche, and rewire our whole process. This shift of consciousness elicits vast growth throughout our soul, so that we become alive through an entirely different fuelling process. Just as we need healthy water-based foods to eat, so we need pranayama to fuel our soul's musculature.

PRAYER AND MEDITATION FOR ZADKIEL'S LOVE

And so let us pray to Zadkiel for the wisdom of God's breath and nourishment.

> *Dear Archangel Zadkiel,*
> *Thank you for your comfort and protection – for the abundance of Divine succour you bestow upon me at this time, that I may be about Holy purpose.*
> *Please allow me to breathe the pure light of the immortal Pranayama, so that my vitality, love and strength may be a means to uplift the lives of my brothers and sisters.*
> *Please fill my AB force with your transcendent faith, allowing me to be a person made new.*

Please help me dissolve any thought of stress or fear, uplifting me instead to that place of inner peace which reflects the light of the Source, and where all is love and joy.

Please journey through my life awakening the glory of gratitude within my heart and soul so that I may be thrilled by the gifts of spirit you promise to flood our lives with.

And so it is

Amen

MEDITATION TO DRAW IN ZADKIEL'S HEALING

- Find yourself in your sacred space, whether this be a natural land-scape or your own personal sanctuary, and feel yourself within the presence of the Holy.
- Light a turquoise candle, burn sage essence – Zadkiel's scent – and play soft, ambient music to prepare opening your tenth Chakra for Zadkiel's loving comfort and protection.
- Breathing deeply (please start by initially breathing out the breath from your body), imagine a Larimar/Turquoise Orb emerging from your Tenth Chakra … Breathe this Orb throughout your sanctuary, healing the sanctuary and invoking Zadkiel's presence.
- If you can, place a piece of Larimar in your hand if you are seated with your spine aligned or, if lying down in a supine position, lay the stone between your heart and throat Chakras.
- Align your spine, feel grounded, and be vigilant to receive Zadkiel's healing energy throughout the pulsations and wave energies of your body.
- Breathe wide and deep seven times, feeling the breath as a Larimar force moving through the whole of your spine, through your tenth Cosmic Heart Chakra, and then upwards and beyond into the Cosmos to touch Uranus, Zadkiel 's home planet.
- Pause for some time feeling the stillness and witnessing Zadkiel's presence moving through your sanctuary.
- Then again breathe wide and deep, and this time sound *HI* seven times through the Cosmic Heart Chakra that lies between your Heart and Throat Chakras.
- This will draw Zadkiel's presence even closer to you to create a connection with the comforting, protecting essence of this great Archangel's being.

- Rest... Soak In the Stillness of the Soul and notice how your energy field has spread widely from your body, touched by Zadkiel's Larimar presence.
- Listen to the oracular whisperings of Zadkiel's magic full of divine comfort and love concerning your unique presence on Planet Earth.
- Observe how your whole being has reached a profound state of super-coherence between your head and your heart, between rational thought and the intuition of your soul.
- Identify what your soul says to you about the resolution of a dilemma, a question you may have about moving forward, or a query concerning a societal challenge that may be concerning you.
- Namaste

Gandhi said: *Be the change you want to see in the world*: When we allow this in our lives, we truly begin to live the revolution we may live right now – thus we awake to rebalance 'heart thinking' and 'head feeling'.

Gently holding this possibility in the forefront of our minds means we create a neo-paradigm that leads us to global coherence. Already we can see the proof of this as more and more people turn to meditation, yoga, and other complementary health regimes. These arts bring us to goodly nutrition, contemplation, a belief in physical excellence, and prayerful meditation, which of course infuse our spirituality with divine elixir. Thus we create a counter-revolution to the accelerated stress levels created.

Meditation amplifies our consciousness, and lets us live our divine self. When this occurs, our psyche allows us to see how intuition is the super-highway where the Angels roam. Living thus means the great Orb Wanderers step in to help coordinate our thoughts with the mind of God, and so thinking becomes completely and transparently aligned with our core vibration.

Please say three times, and feel the coherence that it brings:

> I'm safe, I'm secure, all is well,
> And I'm in complete connection with my core vibration.

BEING WITHOUT YOUR CORE VIBRATION

If we live without connecting to our core vibration, we can feel plundered by the negative emissions of the world, and become chaotically imbalanced as the Ego Mind takes over. This means that our AB energy dwindles, holding us in challenging patterns so that the material illusions of life appear to be all there is. When we feel there is no connection with the Divine, the challenges heap high, and in a bewildered state we yell at God or curse under our breath: *"Why are you doing this to me? Why is God punishing me?"*

This of course is absurd because God isn't doing anything to us, but rather we are creating the challenge for ourselves. Whatever this may be, whatever the circumstance, whatever the vicissitude, God isn't making our lives miserable. Rather, through profound benevolence, God has let us decide what our fate is. Through the flexibility of free will, through the nature of the wisdom of uncertainty, through the versatility of the law of two by which we comprehend nothing is singular, everything is plural, through the purpose of thought and feeling combined – we fashion our own destiny.

It is by the light of our destiny that we caress enlightenment into creation, and it is through conscious spiritual practice that our vibration lifts to higher vibrations. Trying to create by deluding ourselves isn't enlightened. Enlightenment is wholly believing and utterly experiencing a continual sense of embodiment in response to the truths of life.

Rumi gave us an exquisite reminder of this, believing that when enlightenment occurs:

> *The time has come to turn your heart*
> *Into a temple of fire.*
> *Your essence is gold hidden in the dust,*
> *To reveal its splendour*
> *Is to burn in the fire of love.*

To burn with the deepest desire within the temple of this love means that honesty and truth allow us to reveal the shadow of our deepest, darkest secret. Then, by releasing the shame and hurt, our nature is wholly transformed. Renunciation and Atonement inevitably allow AB energy to evolve, and thus we change the course of our destiny. For the heart is the key that always brings us to the greatest integrity. When listening to the heart, dowsing with the heart, counseling with the heart, loving with the heart, playing with the heart, we create a compass that always decides the best way, the most noble way forward. This path then becomes a divine unfolding.

THERE IS NO SEPARATION FROM THE DIVINE

Believing there is no separation from the Divine fires the deepest desire to create adoringly, because we are alerted to reverence in those moments of divinity, and awe and joy present themselves as gatekeepers to the mystical pathway. Believing in the intense, immense and intimate way the Universe speaks to us brings to account the power and the glory of whom we truly are, not just what we thought we were.

Any question that arises about not being in touch with the power of the Divine simply ceases, so let us dispel questions such as these:

Is God Male or Female?
When I die, will I be judged?
What is it to feel that life is the reality of my existence?
Is illness something that just happens by accident?
Is cancer inevitable?
Are brain tumours incurable?
My body is not able to regenerate on a cellular level, is it?

These questions are immature and historic. Our body may be occupying the same space as our spirit, but our essence is in touch with an entirely different order of experience, a non-local terrain. Everything atomic is composed of an energy that encourages and enthuses its particles to move in harmony. Therefore we have the ability to replace or remove old belief systems for new ones in a trice, and within our localized bodies we have the ability to heal all phenomenon by connecting with God's healing energy, with the ALL THAT IS.

The best way to heal is to feel the light of the Source moving through the entirety of our being, as we feel through meditation and prayer. The best way to heal is to feel the vibration of love flowing through your cells. The best way to heal is to revere the nature of your body as a temple for your soul. The best way to heal is by truly recognizing our bodies are hard-wired for health and not disease.

Our bodies are fantastic clusters of cells, a hundred trillion of them vibrating in harmony to achieve our greatest glory. The goal is simple, to optimize our creative energy full of love and joy. We are from the Source, and this superlative field of interconnectivity is an infinitely unfolding creative possibility, full of similar star-seeds, full of love and joy. Espousing these verities opens the vault of your heart where the keys to paradise are found and so we ascend. Resourcing life thus means we become better people, full of exciting loving fire.

AB – THE GRATITUDE OF THE HEART OPENING TECHNIQUES

There exists a series of quintessential questions we may ask of ourselves, to check the probity of our hearts in preparation for the 'weighing of the heart ceremony'. These were initially entered in my book *The Heart's Note* and they have helped many people to scour their integrity for lies within.

Questions like these measure the mortal heart and the immortal soul. They are substantive ways of considering the everyday action of our heart, and by responding to their vitality we literally become more creatively embodied; moving from the head to the heart:

> Do you feel that your heart is heavy with burden?
> Do you feel that your heart is alight with life?
> How often do you act compassionately to yourself?
> How often do you act compassionately to others?
> Have you consciously eliminated defensive anger in your life?
> Are appreciation and gratitude keys to your living?
> Do you make life choices with your heart?
> Are you mawkishly sentimental in the use of your heart?
> Do you love to give and receive through life?
> What work do you engage in to alleviate the suffering of others?
> Are you lovingly healing the 'Heart Stabs' of life?
> Do you consciously celebrate the 'Heart Tingles' of life?

As these questions penetrate deeply, allow a full evaluation to occur, for they will bring such awareness to your heart, and you will feel encouraged to always make conscious choices with your heart. Inevitably, this will bring the strategy of heartfelt action through doing and being/giving and receiving into every moment of each day. All that you require is a belief that love exists as the central premise within the core presence of the Cosmos.

Living life fully from your heart means creating each choice with your heart and, by so doing, be present to the sanctity of each moment. For when we stop considering the NOW of each breath, we've moved too fast through life, in the attempt to accomplish the superfluous tasks that often fill our lives with nothing but action.

Conversely, the inspirational force of the Universe has a fundamental loving presence that pervades through all existence. This force supports us unconditionally and allows us to recognize that as a child of God we are all abundant, and completely loved. Therefore, any external abundance we may reap is a reflection of who we are.

True prosperity is the fostering of our spirit in the service of love, and is upheld and lovingly fostered by the fellowship of the Divine Feminine, some of whom exist in flesh today and some who have returned to spirit – we are lovingly supported by Isis, Hathor, Mother Mary, Quan Yin, the Magdalene, Mother Teresa, Diana, Ammachi, Gurumai, Mother Meera and Maat.

MAAT – THE BRINGER OF TRUTH, THE GUARDIAN OF AB

Maat was the ancient Egyptian Goddess of truth, justice and harmony, and the wife of the God Thoth – the God of wisdom and the principal Scribe of the Gods. Maat was pre-eminent in ancient Egypt as the hallowed giver and receiver of life, and her eternal emblem was the ostrich feather of truth – she was known as the guardian of veracity. Maat used this feather at the weighing of the heart ceremony, as the individual heart consciousness of the departed one was weighed against the weight of the feather by the scales of truth, and in the Halls of Maat.

This is an illustration of the classic life review process we find in most spiritual doctrines, and is evoked in this writing to be given back to humanity, so that the harmony of the heart can once more fully live.

The personal song of Maat as she weighed the heart was the 'Declaration of Innocence' and was a significant part of the famous *Egyptian Book of the Dead* – an august text designed to fully perceive the purity of the heart in all its wonder, when the declaration was spoken in front of the forty-two judges within the Halls of Maat.

The personal mantra of Maat was her key maxim: to treat others as one would be treated – and so she reigned, or indeed reigns over all of us, with an open heart, brimming with unconditional love, and guiding us towards rightfulness.

In the ancient texts, the primeval sea gives RA instruction to *"Inhale Maat and raise her to your nostrils, so that your heart may truly live."* The inspiration of creation is the great dance of life, which reaches harmoniously throughout all of nature, and therefore Maat carries the harmonic balance between mind, body and soul, specifically conveyed through the heart.

THE AB-HEART CEREMONY

To truly elicit the AB force of the heart, to completely draw its force from the heart into the other light bodies, it is essential to engage in the Egyptian ceremony of the 'Forty-Two Doorways' – acknowledging the principles of the forty-two judges, feeling their influence in our lives literally giving us an opportunity to turn our hearts over, as we weigh their might, seeing where our purity lies.

In ancient Egypt, as in the other cultures pioneered by the Atlantian settlers post the Diaspora, this ceremony was attended by Thoth, Anubis, Maat and Osiris, and so if you have a statue or photograph of any of these four great beings, please draw them in, so that they may be close to your energy, and consecrate your ritual with their unique presence. The following Meditation acts like a *Confessional:*

- Make sure you have **Silence, Solitude and Stillness**.
- Move to your enchanted sacred space, whether this be in nature or in your own beautiful home.
- Dim the lights, burn incense; play muted sacred music that elevates the vibration you wish to create, all of which consecrates the space with a divine countenance.
- Make sure you switch off information technology.
- Find somewhere to sit with an aligned spine – feel the weight of your body with your feet earthed, and your back long.
- Breathe out all your force and relax, then breathe in the healing light of the Universe… feeling the Holy Prana as a brightly coloured silver light moving through the whole of your body relaxing you, creating stillness, healing anything that isn't integrated… Do this three times, letting your body sink deeper and deeper into ease.
- Then be aware of the presence of your Guides, the Gods and Goddesses, and the forty-two Egyptian Judges – who will gift you release from any of your peccadilloes or sins.
- Then say: "I come to thee, oh Holy Ones, in love, humility and truth, to wash clean my errors, and to protect this hallowed space from any evil doing."
- "Dear **Heart**, you who were first opened by my Mother, please do not stand as a witness against me, please do not oppose the Sacred Ones, please do not be hostile in the presence of Holy Maat."
- "Oh Shining Ones – please know I have not committed errors against the Holy of Holies."
- "Please know I have not stolen."
- "Please know I have not killed my brothers or sisters."
- "Please know I have not sabotaged myself, or afflicted anyone else."
- "Please know I have never committed greed, or misused my power over others."

- "Please know I have not claimed ownership over any land of Gaia, over any person, or over what is dear RA's."
- "Please know I have not pretended to be that which I am not. I have not purposely distorted truth to make myself feel better."
- "Please know I have not wasted food, caused hunger in another, or fed from the energy of others, and I have not denied myself nourishment."
- "Please know I have not uttered curses."
- "Please know I have not committed adultery, in thought and word or deed, and I have lived truth."
- "Please know I have made no one weep."
- "Please know I have not selfishly manipulated another for my own ambition or gain. I have not lived my life in the fear of being right or wrong."
- "Please know I have not attacked anybody, or abandoned my connection to God."
- "Please know I have not deceived myself or others. I have not thought myself better or less than others."
- "Please know I have not manipulated or schemed to get what is not mine."
- "Please know I have not been an eavesdropper, or discussed another's secrets shared in confidence. I have not made promises I cannot keep!"
- "Please know I have not slandered nor put anyone down. I have not judged."
- "Please know I have not been angry or self-righteous without a just cause."
- "Please know I have not done anything to manipulate or break up a partnership."
- "Please know I have not polluted myself."
- "Please know I have not terrorized anyone or caused them to become fearful."
- "Please know I have not lived my life in ignorance of the divine order, and I have not lived in down trodden-ness."
- "Please know that I have not allowed my darkness to be projected onto another, nor have I wanted to hurt anyone, or myself."
- "Please know that I have not closed my eyes or ears to the truth."
- "Please know that I have not defiled the substance of my love, or taken the Divine within me into darkness."

- "Please know that I have not been violent to any other being, and not to myself."
- "Please know that I have not given myself to be a 'Strife Stirrer'."
- " Please know that I have not acted with impatience, desperation or undue haste."
- "Please know I have not sought to control or be invasive with my fellow human beings."
- "Please know I have not spoken unfairly or unnecessarily, for I have not gossiped, and I haven't broken sanctified silence from fear."
- "Please know I have wronged no one, and have not committed any evil acts, or have created guilt in myself or any other."
- "Please know I have not used spells against anybody."
- "Please know I have never consciously stopped the flow of truth, nor denied its expression, and I have never stayed silent when truth needed to be called forth.
- "Please know I have never raised my voice absurdly, or acted small to hide my light."
- "Please know I have always taken responsibility for my actions, and have not abused the name of God, whilst being in victim mode."
- "Please know I have not been arrogant, or ignored the needs of others."
- "Please know I have not separated my humanity from my divinity, or have defended myself knowingly."
- "Please know I have not dishonoured another's gifts, and have not kept for myself the gift that needs to be with the Divine."
- "Please know I have not dishonoured the purity of my child within, and have allowed the innocence of my inner child to shine with-out."
- "Please know I have not destroyed the animal, vegetable or mineral kingdom, or dishonoured the Devic realm."
- "Please know I have searched to reveal my Divinity in each aspect of my life."
- "Dear **Heart**, please see that I am pure, I am pure, I am pure. Please allow the Forty-two Judges to witness my Humility, as I hold firm to the conviction of my love, and affirm the forty-two aspects of the realm of purity, that my love be the means to create further purity. O Judges of my heart, please be witness to my purity, and receive my **Confession** with the strength that I pledge it to you. **Amen**."

- Pause and be silent with the energy that lives throughout the hallowed nature of this space, and notice how your soul is nourished by the unseen Watchers.
- Feel how your heart is suspended in the power of Thoth, Anubis, Osiris and Maat and, as they respond to your pledges, know that your intention was utterly pure.
- When it is finished, be grateful to the space, and all that has happened, knowing that you are a completely different person than you used to be!
- Namaste

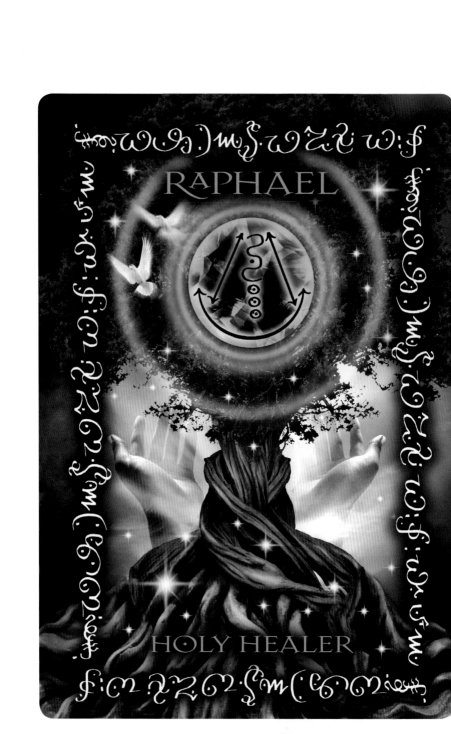

SEVEN

†HE BA

*To accept your spiritual potential is to accept
God's love deep in the core of your being.*

– A COURSE IN MIRACLES

The BA is the essence of the I AM PRESENCE made manifest in human form, and mirrors the sacred energy of the AB. This union signifies a Divine marriage, when the joy of the human heart marries with the love of the celestial soul and, each time this occurs, there sounds in heaven a rapturous chorus of *Halleluiah*, specifically created by the Angels of Atlantis. Each time this occurs, human discernment unifies with divine reasoning.

> *When God gives this agreement, it cannot be taken away.*
> *When God lets us create this union, its infinite potential cannot be*
> *taken away.*
> *When God grants us this readiness to love, it cannot be taken away.*

The I AM PRESENCE evokes the principle of God's essence emerging from Heaven, and revealing celestial form in each one of us, which is BA. We are each in a direct relationship with God because He has placed a portion of Himself within us. This portion is a vibrant mixture of our unconditional love and inestimable joy, where the vital element of the I AM coda celebrates the meeting between eternity and linear time in flesh. Therefore, living fully in the present, living completely in the presence of the I AM, means there is simply no place for the trappings of the ego. God lives within us and, in each moment, gives sway to the fact that the past and future are nowhere, except in our minds. God gives us all of the **Now**!"

> *When God gives us the opportunity to perceive change, that cannot*
> *be taken away.*
> *When God lets us see that we are wrapped by and within the*
> *inner-folds of eternity, that cannot be taken away.*
> *When God grants us the power to live in the infinite light of His*
> *abundance, that cannot be taken away.*

The coda of the I AM was first seeded in time immemorial, and illustrated in the story of Moses communicating with God via the burning bush – the bush being that beautiful part of nature through which God shows Himself.

God is reported to have said: I AM THAT I AM [Exodus 3:14] when Moses asked "What should I refer to you as being?" Since that time, the coda has been used as a key, or sonic glyph, as a sacred talisman to enter the existence of a self-realized human form meeting God essence in eternity.

I AM THAT I AM means, *I have timeless being, I am timeless through eternity.*

PRAYER FOR THE I AM THAT I AM – EHYER ASHER EHYEH

The Angels of Atlantis have given us a second (like the prayer in Chapter Five) I AM prayer-poem to use, whereby we may move even more deeply into the presence of the great I AM PRESENCE of the Cosmic Mind.

- Please move into the veneration of your soul's presence in the space where you are, whether this be in town or country.
- Feel the Shining Ones around you.
- Ground your being, seeing the silver pranic cord moving through your whole spine into Mother Earth, and then subsequently off into the Cosmos. Link with Sister Planet Venus, seeing her over-shadowing this Temple.
- Let your breath release by blowing out and, when ready, breathe in through your nostrils, seeing the breath as silver light, filling your body from top to toe.
- See the breath light, the sacred pranayama, fill your whole body.
- Then Chant *OM* through your heart seven times to consecrate this Holy Instant
- Then say or chant the following prayer:

HYMN TO THE 'I AM' OF THE BA

I AM abundant life for evermore
I AM abundant love and joy for eternity
I AM celestial, everywhere made manifest
I AM the alpha and omega – the first and the last
I AM all peace in the still small voice of the calm

I AM the divine spark of love
I AM eternal youth and beauty
I AM a limitless essence
I AM the source of all life and all intelligence
I AM the currency of love and light

I AM grace
I AM playful laughter
I AM all beauty in Nature
I AM the innocence of faith
I AM

I AM hope
I AM the transcendent principle of the eternal Masters
I AM the lover giving life to all
I AM the healing presence
I AM the illimitable light

I AM the Kingdom
I AM the Power
I AM the Glory
I AM forever and ever
I AM LOVE – AMEN

- Rest in the holy instant of **Now** feeling how the wonderment of the profound soul of the Cosmos soaks within your body.
- Feel the silent peace and the still calm in the space around you.
- With all your heart's love and intelligence, thank God for this moment of bliss!

PRAYER FOR GRATITUDE

Dear Angels,
Thank you for these cherished moments.
Thank you for your ineffable love.
Thank you for the trusting light that you bestow.
Thank you for reminding me of the infinite intoxication of faith.
Thank you for believing in me when my path has veered from belief.
Thank you for granting me the grace to be your vessel and to serve the world.
Thank you for allowing me to become what you would have me be.
Thank you for showing me how to do what you would have me do.
I give my love to your cascading presence....

THE SOUL'S ETERNAL PRESENCE

The BA has no allegiance to weight, space or time because it is an absolute connection point with the Source. The BA literally morphs into being the embodied soul anchored within the heart and, as such, allows a rare quality of integration to take place, orientating a path to the higher levels of spiritual attainment, those which consort with the celestial realms. This quality of discernment permits elevation to the higher octaves of the immortal universal soul, that that we call the **Eternal Presence**. The eternal means the never-ending present through which God lives and is always true.

All things that are most true are eternal. Yet being thus does not refer to a point in time when death occurs on the physical plane. Rather it defines a moment-oriented reality that lives forever as a continuum. Civilizations rise and fall, yet moral maxims like love and truth pervade, for love is built forever, and truth arises from the absolute. Yet the building in which you sit will crumble, it is guaranteed, for all conditions are temporary!

In a speech that Queen Elizabeth the Second gave to the Church of England Synod in 2010, she said: *When so much is in flux, when limitless amounts of information, much of it ephemeral, is instantly accessible and on demand in our world, there is a renewed hunger within our people for that which endures and gives meaning.*

The songs we sing
Are like foam on the
Surface of the sea of being,
Whilst the precious gems we sing of,
Lie deep beneath.
The tenderness in
The songs is a reflection
Of what is hidden in the depths.

Stop the flow of your words,
open the window of your heart,
And let the soul speak.

– RUMI

What is true is that our lives are immersed in technology, and yet in the same instant, ravished by our need for the soul of the sacred, we seek out that, that endures and gives meaning. We seek out transparent credibility, we seek out integrity, we seek out love, we seek the landscape of the inspired epic – for these great stories alert our imaginations, open our hearts, provide us with the quest for truth, and summon us to salve our lives by drenching them in the knowledge and the wisdom of the timeless.

The consequential and essential elements of our mythic past and archetypal consciousness open before us on the page, or on the screen: dazzling, evocative, gut wrenching, heart palpating, and powerfully educative. They often speak of a time that is no more, although increasingly movies are set in the future. Yet, whichever modus is used, whatever time frame informs us, these precepts exist for time immemorial. One such compass is that love as a vibration lasts forever and, by its beauty, propagates peace, kindness and compassion.

THE SOUL OF THE WORLD

Martin Luther King said: *The arc of the moral compass in the Universe may be long, but it always bends towards justice.* Justice, honesty, truth, integrity, and probity are qualities that always persevere. They lead us to know the illusion of linear time, for they show us where the eternal now begins. They lead us to faith, hope and charity, the bedrock of our earthliness.

The moral precepts of faith, hope and charity, of love, peace and joy, appear in the universal popularity of magical films such as *The Lord of the*

Rings, Harry Potter, Avatar, The Water-Bender – movies that not only inspire, but also bring back the magic that has been missing in our lives. They restore our belief in the sacred, for within the story line lives those aspects of our lives that wish to endure. They restore our belief in prophecy, and they reconnect us with truths that are so worth breathing deeply for.

Through distrust in the dogma of religion, we turn to the inspired epic, to the imagination of the great story, to rebalance our morality. The archetypal field of the collective unconscious – the kingdom of the imaginal – is where the light rests closely with the dark, shoulder to shoulder – the yin and yang, the constrictions and the freedoms, the flow and the resistance, our courageous progressions and our dwindling constitutions – they all rest as one.

Further still, the mythic archetypes of our epic tales provide us with powerful keys into our consciousness, enabling us to develop and sustain the deeper aspect of our nature when everything else appears to fall.

In 1963 President Kennedy alluded to the power within the works of art created by the great epic or lyric stories:

> *When power leads man toward arrogance, poetry reminds him of his limitations.*
> *When power narrows the areas of man's concern, poetry reminds him of the richness and diversity of his existence.*
> *When power corrupts, poetry cleanses, for art establishes the basic truths, which must serve as the touchstones of our judgment.*

THE TOUCHSTONES OF DIVINE REASONING

It is the touchstones of our human discernment, and the lodestones of our divine reasoning, that lead us forth to glory, particularly during this present period of amazing growth. During this time on our planet, nobody can feel good about holding back their magnificence. Today, unlike our forebear's allegiance to the patriarchal construct of "they know best", expressing our individual potential is not just our God-given right, it is our job, it is our responsibility. For as we glory in our optimized creativity, so we give opportunity for everyone to do the same.

Conversely, if we dwell on our limitations, if we just keep thinking in minimal ways, we restrict ourselves to a point of disbelief in our own ineffable glory, and that of the Universe. If we don't believe in the infinite possibility of universal abundance full of love and joy, we stop ourselves from experiencing the miracles that God has in store for us.

Why would we wish to deny ourselves the gifts of God? Why would we wish to be dressed in the trappings of the Ego? Why would we wish to be suppressed by the servitude of the obsequious? Why would we wish to take the path of the mediocre or the oppressed? Why would we hold back from fulfilling the divine wisdom of our soul relinquishing its karma, and ascending?

Weight, space and time are not what they appear to be, for we choose to be in flesh in order to optimize our creativity, and thence have the opportunity to become the master/mistress of our own destiny, and not to be fixed by the material world. It takes an effortlessly clear person to live this strength, a person who refuses to be full of sentimentality, self-pity and regret; who gets themselves together even when they don't feel particularly ready for life; who goes to the next job interview even if the last six have appeared as rejections. It takes the heavenly gift of grace not to blame an intimate or a colleague when challenging circumstances arise. It takes the wisdom of a spiritual initiate to realize that, no matter how bleak a situation can appear, it is a base from which the trajectory of miracles can occur.

If we are to choose these pathways of liberation, if we are to walk the path to glory, if we are to feel the pulse of our divine blueprint, we must register with God that we're ready for miracles. Universal wisdom states that if we show up with our best achievement, and in our best array, we also show that we believe in the Source and are in complete acceptance of its absolute abundance. What we feel and how we present ourselves always affects our material circumstances – in myriad ways!

What's really extraordinary about the marriage we have with the Source is that the Universe is blueprinted to begin anew in each moment. It is only our negative thinking that stops the Universe from giving us the abundance that is truly miraculous. Miracles occur when we ask God to intervene, and then universal force distorts the space-time continuum, providing us with such gifts of spirit.

All we need do is to be clear about what we wish to create, having atoned our karma, and allowing God to transform our fear. Then, God's will, rather than our own will, creates a new, freshly made holy instant, rich with abundant glory, and pregnant with the very love essence of the now-ness of now.

MIRACLES MAY ABOUND

One evening, some time ago, I was invited to a party with a wonderful *Swami* whom I worked with in London. Swamiji was being entertained by loving Greek devotees, who had ample wealth and abundance, and who chose to give the Holy Man a party post *Darshan*. Darshan is a sacred meeting when devotees gather to receive holy blessing from the Sacred One or Guru, often touching his or her feet in veneration, and receiving *vijboiti* anointment in return. I attended a number of these meetings for Swamiji, and they were absolutely delightful, being in the presence of someone who radiated tremendous love and light.

On this particular occasion, Swami had been invited to this special dinner party with a few of his devotees to celebrate Swamiji's unique ministry. However, the word got out that a party was occurring for this splendid man, and an extra fifty or sixty people arrived at the house in a salubrious area of town.

Of course, the hosts were totally dumbfounded, as they had only prepared a certain amount of food for the few. However, Swamiji intercepted, asking a number of us to join him in the kitchen to chant a mantra with him. We did this, and although no extra food was prepared, literally everybody was fed. In other words, the magic of manifestation was created by Swamiji, just as Yeshua had fed the five thousand with five loaves and two fish all those years ago [Matthew 14: 13-21].

Once, this wonderful man also manifested a beautiful ring for me – out of thin air he produced a gold ring covered in diamonds in the shape of the sacred syllable of the *OM* – as I had seen him manifest other keep-sakes for many faithful devotees. These tokens anchor one in faith, allowing the belief in miracles to pervade throughout one's entire being, so that the idea of the miraculous literally becomes an experience!

We read of miracles in the Holy Bible when Yeshua brings the dead back to life, walks on water, and turns water into wine. In other stories, we hear of God parting the Red Sea, bringing forth Manna from heaven, and encouraging Moses to strike his staff on a rock to bring forth water – on each occasion to save the lives of the chosen few, the Israelites, who were marching from captivity into the promised land.

Jesus said in the Gospel according to St John: *"He that believeth in me, the works that I do, shall he do also, and greater works than these shall he do."*

Miracles occur when we ask God to intercept in our lives, recognizing the BA or Soul as a fragment of the Divine. Miracles occur when He distorts the three dimensions through which we exist, and fuses past and future into one. These are hallowed moments, which elicit a vast and radical power used for healing, restoring, nurturing and regenerating the abundant force of the Source within us, and through the nature our planet.

All we need to do is to turn up for loving, all we need do is to enter with grace in our hearts, all we need do is to send forth rays of belief, faith and trust – for these are three concomitants of love – and then allow faith to saturate our believing. For in Matthew 17:20 it is written: *If ye have faith as a grain of mustard seed, ye shall say unto this mountain, remove hence to yonder place, and it shall remove, and nothing shall be impossible unto you.*

When our faith is as confident as His, when our faith possesses the audacity that moves mountains and parts seas, when we see ourselves clearly as radical revolutionaries adjoined to the call of spiritual arousal, so will we achieve wonders! For truth be spoken, all we need do is turn up in the present, asking, believing and receiving. Then the Universe does the rest, unfolding in the direction of exquisitely empowered goodness. And you know that, within all of this divine, purposeful juggling, the Archangels turn up to do their very best to help us all, for they vibrate the consciousness of love for love's sake.

ARCHANGEL RAPHAEL OVERSHADOWS YOUR BA

The BA soul force is protected and overshadowed by the extraordinary emerald green Orb presence of Archangel Raphael. Raphael arises as the Holy Healer of the soul made flesh and, in this context, 'healing' means a movement back to wholeness, a shift back into core vibration. Raphael as the Angel of Empathy aligns us fully in those hallowed moments, when miraculous healing expands every cell, and each aspect of our lives is edified by divine perfection.

When we beseech Raphael for benediction, the blessing always comes with a sweetness of touch and fullness of allure which draw us into our interior domain, the supreme place where ultimately all is well, and where all negativity is transformed. That place is the secret chamber of the heart – eternal, sublime, and absolute in the conviction of its love. For this is the seat of the soul, and therefore reflects the soul of the God, as this is the sacred part of Him who gave us life!

When we beseech Raphael for healing, we are not only healed, we are vitally attuned to the frequency of the great love light circuitry. This is the very AB force of the Cosmos, which streams through the crystalline grid of our planet, the greater grid of all planetary organisms, and the massive Mother/Father Cosmos itself. Raphael eternally emits an emerald ray of empathetic inspiration in loving care of the natural world and all beings that live a sentient existence.

Thus, Raphael's existence encourages us to watch over the creation of that rare communion between the planet and our earthly nature. Healing in this sense means that we cleanse ourselves, through the cycles of evolution established by our lives, and the planet's evolutionary position within the Galaxy. We then know that healing is a movement back to wholeness, and determine that this is not a random universe, and everyone is wherever they need to be through their divine assignment.

Through Raphael's loving care, we begin to see that there is meaning in everything that occurs, as this is so for the nature of Emerald, a stone used for its healing properties throughout the sands of time. In the Bible, there is reference to the Throne of God being exclusively made of Emerald; in Ancient Egypt, Thoth influenced his Priest-scribes to compose the sacred text of the Kybalion on tablets of Emerald, and old legends have it that an Emerald in a shape of a bowl fell off Satan's crown, and this bowl much later was used by Jesus or Yeshua at the last supper, and that Joseph of Arimathea caught Christ's blood from the cross in this same bowl, founding the order of the Holy Grail.

As the beautiful green of the Emerald reflects Raphael's rays, it is also the colour of the Heart Chakra, a colour that brings unity from opposition, peace from conflict, and healing from strife. Emerald uplifts man from wrongdoing, and heals through calm contemplation. Emerald significantly communicates or reflects the sacred intention within the essence of all that heals. Emerald is the vibration that attuned to the harmony of the natural world and the welfare of all souls in the Devic realms.

OUR DIVINE MISSION

Committing ourselves to soul maintenance, aligning ourselves with the trajectory of our incarnation, becoming a vessel for the Divine light, means we discover our soul's purpose. Of course, this means we experience life as a gift of grace, and so we feel our heart's secret chamber as the seat of the soul and in direct alignment with the Divine Matrix.

Finding our soul purpose means we find the courageous will of SEKHEM to carry us through, to fulfill the course of our Humanity. Throughout much of our lives as initiates, we learn to identify and release the patriarchal restrictions imposed during the saturation of our early lives, through education, and heal the wasteland as we go. Then we turn to transmuting the thousand natural shocks that flesh is heir to, drawing out the arrows of outrageous fortune.

Then, in celebration for the journey thus far, we turn to the greater truth of our soul's purpose that hitherto remained shrouded by the aneasthesia of our soul downloading into these Earthly dimensions, the divine amnesia that brought about a loss of memory of whom you are, and where you came from.

One of the most salient considerations of the awakened soul is to determine what you came here to do. This means we keenly interpret and become very clear about the specific reasons for why we chose the physical form we resplendently live in; why you chose the extraordinary family you were born into; what your Mother, Father and siblings bring to you as gifts, even when this appears not to be the case; why you chose the nature of the country location, society or culture in which you were born, or subsequently were taken to by the unfolding nature of your destiny; why you have chosen the profession, job or field of operation you are engaged in.

The answers to these questions, this consequential knowledge, will spark a deep fire within your soul, guiding your life in the direction of your BA, and allowing you to perceive the dimensional portals within your soul, in order to turn your attention to your highest potential. So here are the significant questions you may ask of yourself:

- Why did my soul choose my Mother and Father?
- Why did my soul choose my siblings?
- Why did my soul choose the members of the extended family?
- Why did my soul choose the location where I was born?
- Why did my soul choose the country or landmass on which I was born?
- Why did my soul choose the nationality of my birth?
- Why did my soul choose the mother tongue of my birth?
- Why did my soul choose the physical nature or circumstance of my birth?
- Where do I feel my soul is from?
- Do I feel in coherence with my family?
- Do I feel in harmony with my chosen career or work?
Am I living my live in total synergy with my soul?

Then, here are further questions you may ask of your self or your soul, for they prompt answers that my arise as extrapolations of your personal circumstances:

- Why has my soul chosen the sexuality I live and love?
- Why has my soul chosen the qualities of my personality?
- Why has my soul chosen the propensities that I seem to have?
- Why has my soul chosen the career or work choices I've made?

- Why has my soul chosen the maturation process that I've been through?
- Why has my soul chosen the conscious choices that I've made?
- What does my soul want as I bring my unconscious world into vision?

As you ask these questions of yourself, plan to also discuss them with a favored counselor, so that you compose a highly accurate picture of yourself. In turn, this will stimulate a powerful identity check of whom you are right now, and how you wish to be – the way you wish to live your soul in the world. Here is a poem the Angels gave us to help us see the simplicity of our soul's sojourn, and how this is a time of immense soul-stride:

THE SOUL WISH OF THE BA

You have come this far
Keep moving…
Keep creating…
Keep loving…
Don't turn back!

You have come to reckon your Soul
Keep observing…
Keep smiling…
Keep loving…
And don't turn back!

Only you hold the true measure of your own success or undoing. Only you know your Soul as it remembers the meaning of your Life, Death & Resurrection.

And so, at this portal to eternity, gather together the vital pieces of you.

Release all the masks of your own making, and remember the music of your wild song, writing its tune, the note of your name, high on the skies!

Know that every tumble, and every turn on the twisting path of life, is a beautiful dance of the living elements that comprise of you.

Every gesture, every thought, every kiss, every smile, every hello and goodbye, is a star scattered on the sanctuary of your soul, as on the firmament of Heaven.

You have come this far…
Keep moving…
Keep creating…
Keep loving…
Keep joying…
And don't turn back!

– THE ANGELS OF ATLANTIS

ARE YOU ACTIVATING YOUR SOUL IN THE WORLD?

Is every breath you take, is every pulse you feel, is every step you take, is every action you make, is every thought you have, is every perception you communicate, is every word you speak, is every deed you conjure, is every feeling you express, is every sense you possess…an action of your soul?

SOUL BIO-IDENTITY CHECK

- Are you living in Faith or Fear?
- Are you living a life generated by the Source of your individual soul and collective soul?
- Are you pulsing and breathing each moment as a Sorcerer?
- Are you living the present moment presence of complete self-awareness, in relation to your core vibration?

- Are you choosing inspiration over desperation for each moment's living?
- Are you living each thought, word and deed as a linguistic suffused with fear or faith?
- Are you feeling yourself in co-creation with your fellow human beings, with the vegetable, animal and mineral kingdoms?

The quieter your mind is, the more you will hear the inner teacher, the Intuition or Inner Tutor communicating with you, and providing the information you need for this humble human discernment process. Then, suddenly, your mind will move from human experiencing to divine reasoning.

Listen to your mind and you will tire of its discourse.
Silence your mind and you will connect with the Source.

–THE ANGELS OF ATLANTIS

THE BA'S PSYCHOLOGICAL ORIENTATION

The more you draw your soul (spirit) and soma (body) into balance, the more you will live in sweet consort with your whole being. In order to not just conceptualize your way forward in using the keys to paradise, in order to fully experience the keys and their might, you need to truly embody all the spiritual principles that they clearly evoke, by feeling each one.

In order to see your spiritual practice not just as an idea but also as an experience, you need to fully ignite your spirit as well as exercise the rational portion of your mind. In order to align with your higher self, you need to rewire your psyche, and refuel your spiritual body through the constant use of mind-altering practices such as prayer and meditation.

We truly begin to cultivate a centre and own the sovereignty of our purpose for being here at a time in our lives when 'experience' searches our soul for truth, when we develop gravitas (gravity); at a time in our lives when an awareness of stillness helps us develop veritas (truth); at a time in our lives when we feel the rhythm of breath fuelling our existence and producing integritas (integrity). Then we absolutely respect meditation and prayer as spiritual exercises that helps us develop specific muscles, which in turn allows us to become stronger, and eventually much more elastic.

When we reach this point in life, gravity has a profound effect on us by pulling us into the Earth in order to examine that which we haven't seen. This is so for our physical musculature, just as it is for our spiritual muscle. For example, feel the lack of muscle strength illustrated in those who are disdainful, cynical, negative, judgmental, controlling, victim oriented or angry – these are dysfunctions arising from a lack of integrity, these are indications of frailty occurring in our spiritual muscle.

If we tone our bodies with the joy-filled gravity of a daily exercise such as Yoga or Tai Chi; if we meditate once or twice a day using sonic meditations dedicated to the substance of our integration in life; if we keep aligning ourselves in all four bodies with the truth of our soulful existence – we release weak musculature and become steadfast about the conviction of our soul's condition.

Here is a sonic meditation that will help you tone your musculature:

THE BA'S SONIC MEDITATION

- Find yourself in your own sacred space, whether this be a natural landscape or your own personal sanctuary.
- Light a green candle, burn Lavender essence (Raphael's scent), and play ambient music to prepare opening a portal for Raphael's

purification of your BA.

- Having sanctified the space, imagine a Green Orb emerging from your Heart Chakra and breathe this Orb throughout your sanctuary, healing the space and venerating Raphael's presence. If you can, place a piece of Emerald or Malachite next to your Fourth Chakra, in your hand or, if lying down in a supine position, lay the mineral literally on your heart.
- Make sure your spine is aligned, feel your feet grounded, and be vigilant to receive Raphael's healing energy throughout the pulsations of your Heart Chakra as the seat of your BA.
- Breathe wide and deep, feeling the breath as an Emerald Green force moving through the whole of your spine, and into the Earth of your physical presence, then upwards and beyond into the Cosmos to touch Orion – Raphael's home planet.
- Pause – then again breathe wide and deep, and this time sound *HAH* seven times through your Heart Chakra – this will draw Raphael's presence closer to you, open your BA further, and promote a feeling of divine love drenching your BA with grace.
- Rest. Soak in the Stillness of the Soul and notice how your energy field spreads around your body, touched by Raphael's Emerald presence. Listen to the oracular whisperings of Raphael's magical presence, full of divine cleansing, communion, Earth and empathy – inspiring you into the centre of your BA's LOVE.
- Sound the *OM* three times.
- Then chant *RA MA DA SAH SAH SAY SO HUNG* several times through each Chakra in an ascending fashion. So start with *RA* in your Base Chakra, and recover the breath on the second *SAH*, so as to move into the Throat Chakra.
- This is the Sacred Heart Mantra, and will fill you full of Cosmic Love.
- **Rest** and feel the subtle magic of this mantra pervade your whole being.

  Its interpretation is this:
  RA – Sun
  MA – Moon
  DA – Earth
  SAH – Soul Infinity
  SAH SAY – Total Infinity
  SO – Personal Merger with the Divine
  HUNG – Infinite Vibration

Now say this prayer to the Infinite Shining Ones:

THE BA'S SONIC PRAYER

Dear God & the Angels,

I wish to serve you with the love of my whole BA.
Please allow me to surrender to you any pains that I may have,
which deny my soul its beauty.
Please may I ask for you to wash clean any fragment of my karma
that holds shadow within my BA.
Please may I surrender to you all lack of clarity, and strive to live
unconditional love.
Please may I use my talents everlastingly in relation to my Earth
Purpose.
Please may I surrender to you all my successes, and all the hopes
that I may have.
Please may I be placed in the circuitry of your everlasting light and
love.
And so it is.
Amen

BA INSPIRATION

Every moment holds a myriad of infinite possibilities, and how much we allow this magnificent force to move through us is determined by our willingness and level of receptivity. If we vibrate on a low-level, we will attract a low frequency of behaviour; if we vibrate at a higher frequency, our lives always attract miracles.

With the miraculous in view, because we believe it to be so, our lives become suffused with new ideas which pop into our minds effortlessly; significant conversations will happen with no overt planning; abundance will flourish in surprising ways; extraordinary people will just pop into your life; then we always appear to be in the right place at the right time.

As these mercies appear, as serendipity occurs, as miracles arrive on our doorstep, this is when we truly need to acknowledge God's intervention, by building an altar to His grace. After all, it's so easy to deify our disasters, forgetting about bringing our blessings to the fore, so much so that our confusions appear to obliterate our need to register this era as a critical time for experiencing one of the greatest soul-strides Homo sapiens has possibly ever made.

Therefore, we must give thanks, and pledge our gratitude for the celestial acceleration occurring in the heavens. This means that each and every one of us must see the inspiration of our BA at the foremost of our consciousness – so we make ourselves absolutely available to the Cosmos; so we turn up in order to seize the opportunity of evolving to the fullness of our divine potential; so we literally arrive to be positioned within the circuitry of God's plan, and we see the world remade in the image of our love.

THE SPIRITUAL VORTEX

Seeing ourselves at the centre of the spiritual vortex of this time signifies that we have the means to constantly retune our core vibration, just as our brothers and sisters also do. Within the vortex – within our core – our BA lies couched in infinite happiness. Indeed, the happiest time of our lives can be when we help others, rather than in doing something just for ourselves. Any perception that harbours a separate sense of need is ultimately based on fear, whereas any perception that embraces all-oneness breeds peace.

In order to move with elasticity throughout the infinite folds of universal creation, in order to bring one's own thinking into alignment with the laws of creation, in order to bring about the manifestation of the law of attraction for the manifold unfolding of your soul's purpose, you need to see that thought creates reality, and feeling actualizes manifestation.

Write down all the things that you hold rich gratitude for, all of those things that you have created and which you hold the Universe in great gratitude for. Loving the Universe with gratitude stimulates the Stars to align you with abundance, for if we do what we love and love what we do, we undoubtedly connect with our core vibration, and this touches the very heart of the universe, because both energies are in sync. Similarly, showing gratitude by sending off rockets of desire turbo boosts the Universe into manifesting your desires with full gusto.

Try these oaths to the Universe, with joy in your mind, love in your heart and deep appreciation in your soul, and creation will appear in the next second. Then please write your own for your specific requests:

A VORTEX OF GRATITUDE

I'm in the spirit vortex and I'm so grateful for my beautiful home.

I'm in the spiritual vortex and I'm so grateful for the unique work that I do.

I'm in the spirit vortex and I'm so grateful for the amazing relationships and friends I have.

I'm in the spiritual vortex and I'm so grateful for my communion with soul & spirit.

I'm in the spirit vortex and I'm so grateful for the Angel's gifts.

I'm in the spiritual vortex and I'm so grateful for the creativity of my I AM PRESENCE.

I'm in the spirit vortex and I'm so grateful for my hobbies.

I'm in the spiritual vortex and I'm so grateful for the abundant possibilities.

I'm in the spirit vortex and I'm so grateful for my beautiful body and health.

I'm in the spiritual vortex and I'm so grateful to feel creation at work.

I'm in the spirit vortex and I'm so grateful for the luxuries of life, for light and beauty.

I'm in the spiritual vortex and I'm so grateful for my love of travel.

I'm in the spirit vortex and I'm so grateful for the being of Mother Earth.

I'm in the spiritual vortex and I'm so grateful for the being of Father Heaven.

I'm in the spirit vortex and I'm so grateful for the food and water that nourish me.

I'm in the spiritual vortex and I'm so grateful for the riches in my life.

I'm in the spirit vortex and I'm so grateful for the wonders that come to me.

I'm in the spiritual vortex and I'm so grateful for the sonic meditations I have.

I'm in the spiritual vortex and I'm so grateful for wonderful conversations.

I'm in the spiritual vortex and I'm so grateful about being with **Love**!

I'm in the spirit vortex and I'm so grateful to the Universe, and all my Spirit Guides.

Being thus within the thrall of Cosmic Creation means we prepare our Ascension Vehicle, through connecting with the BA at a higher-level initiation, one that configures with the Cosmic or Galactic soul.

Indeed, in ancient Egypt, the Pharaoh, as a highly evolved spiritual initiate, would prepare for the Osirification process by engaging in the methodology this book has thus far revealed. Once engaged, he would then be taken to the *omphalos* of the world (the stone navel of the Great Pyramid at Giza) for a highly significant ritual that unified him not only with the Ascension Process of his soul and his incarnation, but also with the collective soul of his people.

THE BA AT EL GIZA PLATEAU

The Pyramids on the Giza plateau at Cairo are three of the most powerful portals on our planet for the Human BA Ascension Vehicle, for they hold planetary co-ordinates with unique star trajectories within the Galaxy.

Indeed, the Pyramids and all the Temples of Ancient Egypt mark astro-geographical locations that configure some of the most unique spiritual sites on our planet – developed in ancient times by the Atlantean culture that first brought their spiritual technology to the area after the cataclysm that destroyed Atlantis.

The Great Pyramid represents the BA of the King God of Paradise – Osiris.

The Second Pyramid represents the BA of the Queen Goddess of Heaven – Isis

The Third Pyramid represents the BA of their son the God Horus

And the Sphinx was the guardian protector of the Giza Plateau, which specifically arose as a formation of Anubis (the God of the Dead) in order to protect both the Osiris and Isis energies, through the unfolding that took place in the Osirification process of the Pharaoh.

The Pharaoh as a spiritual initiate who thought of as an anointed one – a pre-ordained incarnation of the Divine in Human form – would be taken by his Priests to the Giza Plateau, in particular the Great Pyramid, on certain highly auspicious astrological occasions. He would then be led into the Well of the Great Pyramid, where he would meet all his fears, and through alchemy release these forebodings.

He would then rise to the Queen's Chamber where harmonic healing would be given by the High Priests, at which point he would then move to the Kings' Chamber. Here he would transit into the initiation of the Christ Consciousness of the Galaxy, by lying in the stone sarcophagus, and communing with the many planetary constellations that align with the portal of the King's Chamber, through open shafts in the Pyramid.

The Pharaoh would then be taken into the Pyramid of Isis for connection with the womb of the world and, through elevated meditations, would transmute the collective karma of the world, whilst being spiritually held by twelve Priestesses who were specifically trained to hold the collective crises of the world within their wombs, whilst ancient magical rites were used for collective healing.

Finally, the initiate would be taken to the Horus Temple of the third Pyramid, for further rites and meditations which enabled an aspect of the Divine Child within Horus, born of the marriage between Isis and Osiris, to be opened and sanctified into the Homo luminous – the next stage of evolution for human beings. These processes allowed Christos energy to cascade through the pure one, creating a powerful ignition between the meeting of the BA and the KA into the two further light bodies to be awakened by the Angels, namely the SAHU and the AKHU, completing the final stages of the Keys to Paradise.

The ultimate Temple that created an astro-geographical portal for the Egyptian Ascension Process is lost in mystery, hidden by the magic of the ancient High Priests. Yet I would conjecture that this last portal of Ascension is a small Chapel dedicated to Osiris, in the eastern part of the great Temple of Karnak in Luxor – the throat Chakra of the world. Having spent periods of time visiting this chapel, meditating and seeing into its seven keys of life, and its seven doors to heaven, the Angels have taken me on a journey to comprehend its use.

EIGHT

THE SAHU

If there is a definition of refined spirituality, it is the tuning of the heart. Tuning means the changing of pitch of the vibrations, in order that one may reach a certain pitch that is the natural pitch; then one feels the joy and ecstasy of life, which enables one to give pleasure to others even by one's presence, because one is tuned.

– HAZRAT INAYAT KHAN

This eighth key to paradise emits through the power of SAHU, a portal that proclaims we humans are 'something else', with a potency that exudes from the perfection God, which is rich within all of us, whether this be manifest or not. This otherworldly Charisma has a sense of magic that is always available for expression. Each of us is abundant with the might of God's perfection, for that is who we are and nothing else.

SAHU is an exhilarating state of being, where the very temperature of human form merges with the incandescent love-light of the Divine.

SAHU occurs as the light of the Universe becomes one with your physical body, so transfiguring you into an immortal being.

SAHU is the awesome experience of the AB heart energy being drenched by the love that humbly draws you to gently surrender your individual will to meld with that of the Divine.

SAHU is the transcendental state where fusion is created between the power of SA and the force of HU.

SAHU is the celestial breath of the Divine becoming form, for *SA* in ancient Egyptian spirituality signified the breath of life, whereas *HU* represented the continuous flow of breath transformed into sound, which emits itself through the sacred syllable of *OM* in Sanskrit, and the supernal tone of *RA* in Egyptian.

Furthermore, *HU* was the sound of creation, which the great Egyptian God Atum proclaimed as he ejaculated his seeds of creation onto Earth, which then became the nine primary Egyptian Gods and Goddesses.

SAHU HU-MAN BEINGS live fully embodied soul states, vibrating healthy minds and bodies vitally engaged in the prana of breath – essentially centered with aligned spines, living generously in an open hearted way, full of love and joy.

Feeling these sensations – experiencing this state of being – means we literally appear as though we're standing as giants, or standing on the shoulders of giants – the colossi of inspiration and the infinite – for when we exist thus, we literally see much further and, in the flicker of supernal light, we become saturated in a visionary consciousness.

SAHU LIFE lived with awareness of the immortality of the universe is a life that is fully merged with the breath of the infinite Source, and from a mind filled with infinite love arises the power to create infinite possibility. Thinking and feeling in this way means that we attract and amplify all the love in the world. Such ways are called Enlightened.

SAHU LIVES

Some of the most outstanding examples of SAHU transfigured human consciousness existed in the Ascended Ones that now are known as Thoth, Akhnaton, Tutankhamun, Jesus, Mary, Babaji and Sai Baba. These beings once trod the planet living heaven on Earth, as they breathed Divine light into their beings, whilst teaching powerful maxims concerning love and truth, honesty and grace, wisdom and generosity. Transfigured thus, all their blood, water, cells, bones, tissue, musculature, feelings, chakras and DNA, transformed into a lucid state of crystal perfection – wholly refracting the higher frequencies of the love-light circuitry of the Cosmos.

SAHU connects us with an embodied God form, producing a stage of human evolution that merges with the infinite, and unifies us with the light of supernal perfection.

The key to SAHU is breath, for our breath is the literal and metaphoric conduit between matter and spirit. When we synchronize our lives with breath, we expand our consciousness through deeper states of meditation. Thence we access much higher forms of energy that transform the mind-body relationship, altering all of our bio-systems, and eventually allowing us to reach a breathless state of bliss, known in Sanskrit as Samadhi.

Knowing this, living this, we become transfixed by the eyes of God, for in the eyes of the Infinite One we are held to be perfect – shining forth our unlimited capacity for brilliance through an experience of life that pulses love in each instant. We can see this in those who live the miracle of **Shining**. We can see this light radiate out from His Holiness the Dalai Lama, and Aung San Suu Kyi.

Miraculous beings, miraculous happenings, and miracle-based thought, cannot hold the conviction of dishonesty or denial, because miracles are based on love, not fear. Miracles are based on the assumption that only love exists, and therefore no negativity can live where nothing else matters but **Love**.

Living within miracle-based thinking means that the miracle worker doesn't become weighed down by the problems of the world, but rather develops visionary zeal to see through the vicissitudes of life to the light and magic beyond, and thereby creates a world that lies there – the vision that those earlier giants had of inspiration and the infinite.

Through SAHU, through the currency of miraculous thought based on the reality of unconditional love, we are given the strength to turn any situation that lacks love into one that is once again full of loving. This starts by re-conceiving the way we think, this shifts by changing the way our thoughts affect others, this transforms by taking full responsibility for the way we love, this evolves by not holding judgment, lack of forgiveness, or any other negative feeling. Therefore we learn to give up these emotions to the Angels, in order for them to coalesce the force back into their plasma, to be re-cycled into awe.

As a miracle-based thinker, one develops a prophetic voice, derived from the teacher within. This teacher arises from a higher source intervening on our behalf, for intuition is seeing with the soul. This of course means that God got there before we did, because God had already implanted in our genetic membrane the nature of prophetic wisdom – the wisdom of the teacher-guide who always knows how to lead in the direction of love and hope. This teacher is the Higher Self, the Holy Spirit, the Paraclete, the Guardian Angel, a Wise Counsel who brings evolution to the SAHU.

SHAMAEL AND OUR GUARDIAN ANGEL

Our bodies are blueprinted for health, not disease, and so it is our negative thinking and feeling that makes us unwell. Living within SAHU means we draw an even closer supernal teacher to us. This is our Guardian Angel who constantly dispenses miraculous aid from Archangel Shamael, as Shamael is the Divine Guide, the Angel of Hope, the Holy Listener, the Silent Witness – the one who always directs us to the compass of our inner core, the one who holds the beacon of hope that never ceases to wane or lose its shimmering focus, for when the world says give up, Shamael as **Hope** always whispers…"try once more!"

Jesus found this in the garden of Gethsemane during his darkest night, when Shamael provided him with the assurance of loving compassion, so that he could look on his crucifixion with the nature of the resurrection beyond. The vast love of Shamael created a ray of hope that overshadowed the burden of the mortal flesh that shone so brightly in its Lilac Light, that it guided Jesus through his dilemma, gently alleviating his pain with the pure love of heaven.

Likewise, Shamael spreads Angelic force over us during the times in our own lives when colossal change is threatened – the times when bereavement, disease, divorce, internal conflict or work-related resignation occur. These are the occasions when we need to be on bended knee, truly asking Shamael for guidance. Archangelic love always shines forth bringing succour and guidance about which path we most need to take – the path that fulfills the glory of our divine inheritance.

You see, the love that Shamael offers is a love that transcends the ordinary. This is the SAHU love that maneuvers our consciousness through the wastelands of despair into valleys of deep balm, that then again change into extraordinary oases of emotional maturity. Once there, this exquisite Archangel takes from us the horrors of life and strikes the cosmic note of serenity in our souls, so that we may meet the portal of a new beginning.

Shamael with the twelve Angels of Atlantis facilitates the muscle of the miraculous, because they have the power to help miracles spring from the profound intercession of the human soul. This is their dispensation from the Divine for they champion intercession as thoughtful prayer, where we reach to a space beyond our own, bringing light into the darkness.

Intercession is when we take full responsibility for melding our will, with the Divine. You see, underneath the surface layer of normal thought lies a deeper level of consciousness that's filled with pure peace and love. All we need is the action of prayer and meditation to access this, to dig deep into the fiber of our being, to find the stillness that dwells there – the still small voice of the calm. For the more things happen on the outside, the more we need stillness on the inside.

All the mistakes we make in our busy everyday lives create un-centeredness for, in the moment we commit the mistake, we're not living in conscious connection with our core presence, with our inner teacher, our Guardian Angel. Mistakes occur when we aren't centered in core vibration, and so this is why making contact once or twice a day with that special part of our soul, through meditation and prayer, is the singularly most powerful thing we can do.

Count the number of times you've made a mistake that has affected the rest of your life, simply because in the moment of making it you were not present – as you moved too fast through life. This moving too fast occurs as a result of stress, of fear, of habitual behaviour that appears unconscious. Would you have made that mistake if you had been present to remembering who you truly are, a spiritual being on a human journey? Being caught within the miasma of non-presence, being unresolved about who we truly are, being lodged within the negativity of not getting our own way, being proven ineffectual by work colleagues – all these things and more allow us to misperceive who we are.

A few minutes spent each day with the Archangels, with Shamael, with in-tuition, with the Holy Spirit, will guarantee that the inner Teacher-Guide will be with you, guiding the drive of your incarnation, filling your thinking all day. But instead, because we are victim to the Ego, the Ego speaks loudest, and the vibration of the inner teacher is cast aside. For the sage will never impose, but rather must be yielded to and received, having first made space for the knowledge.

There is an ancient Cabbalistic legend concerning Shamael that suggests this is the Archangel who, *binds, bans, and stops the mouths of evil speakers, jealous and wicked judges, emirs, satraps, governors, men of authority, executioners, prefects, the gentile or the infidel. Shamael binds the mouths of all wicked judges, all evil ones; binding all their tongues and lips, their minds and thoughts, their ways and beings.*

The best way to summon your true calling is to place yourself in service to God, and so we see Shamael doing the same, silencing the Ego. Accordingly, if we can just spend a few minutes a day tuning into the Holy Spirit, we can guarantee that the Holy One will be overshadowing our thought process throughout the whole day. Then we release the fetters of the Ego, which loves to claim that we are alone. Instead, in meditation, we recognize we are **all one**, and part of a holy system of consciousness that flows through the inner veins of all things, of everything, but can only be truly perceived if we are aware of being aware: Not that this engenders perfection, but it wakes us to the possibility of miracles, and in a way where we would be so otherwise engaged.

MIRACLES ABOUND

The other day I experienced a miracle. I was processing a particularly challenging conversation with a close colleague, who appeared to be in denial for hurting someone he knew was particularly sensitive to the process we engaged in. Instead of taking full responsibility for the situation, he became aloof to the affect his behaviour had, and I decided to go for a walk in order to pray and to touch the healing balm of Mother Nature – I was simply tired and needed nature's elevation.

Walking at a gentle pace, I asked beautiful Shamael for succour, looked up and, there in the cloudless blue sky, I saw a cloud, burst into the shape of a Heart. I was so touched by its power and beauty, and then the sun hiding behind the cloud, suddenly burst forth its rays. This was absolutely spectacular, and in a trice another smaller heart opened in the centre of the cloud, shining light from within its core. I was speechless with awe, teary-eyed as I felt my question had been answered. And so it had, because not only did I feel more aligned with core vibration, I also knew this love was the face of God.

Through SAHU, God's help always comes when we are bitten by the horror of conflict, the searing shame of bankruptcy, the ignominious divorce, the fear of disease. For our lives to change, we must travel deep. Yet no matter what, there is always – just beyond the grief – an infinite field of possibility where miracles hover, waiting to be dispensed when loving honesty is addressed through prayerful intercession.

PRAYER FOR PEACE

> *Dear Shamael and the Holy Angels of Atlantis,*
> *Please turn the hearts of all people to love.*
> *Please bring the Holy Spirit's light of peace to all nations, cultures, and establishments of our world.*
> *Please allow the foundations of love, truth, and right-mindedness to be the keystones for the healing of our minds and hearts.*
> *Please allow all suffering to cease in the flickering of an eye, bringing forth divine peace.*
> *Please hear my prayer, and let the wondrous Angels bring to us joy and healing from their beautiful hearts.*
> *So be it.*
> *Amen*

THE ANUBIS MEDITATION

- Find **Silence, Solitude and Stillness**, in your sacred space, whether this be your own meditation sanctuary, or a beautiful arbor in nature.

- Burn incense, ring a bell or singing bowl, play sacred music to purify the space, and switch off cell phones or any communication technology that may disturb your meditation.

- Find a comfortable chair in which to sit, or be cross-legged on a cushion if you wish.

- Feel your spine as fully aligned as possible, establishing your spine as the SAHU conductor of your energy, and imagine a deep Indigo or Obsidian laser light shining through your entire spine.

- Follow the Indigo light down through to the base of your spine, through the chair, the floor, the building… into the basement, the Earth's crust, the soil, the clay, the stone, the rock… and into deep bedrock, into the very womb of Mother Earth.

- Sense how Mother Earth receives your force, your call of gravity, for she is always present to hold us in unconditional love – it's just that we forget her.

- See from the end of the Indigo light further filters of light growing like amazing roots, magnificently extending throughout the vast rock, deep beneath you.

- These are the light tendrils of your SAHU's incandescence – a light that seeks connection with Mother Earth and, when in contact, immediately feel her loving elixir spreading through these roots, nourishing your whole physical form.

- Ask Mother Earth for a gift, a vision, a blessing – and then siphon the energy up though the laser of your pranic-cord into your heart's secret chamber. Extend this upwards further, all the way through your spine, up out through your crown chakra.

- Feel the Indigo light extend further, upwards into the expansion of your energy field, and then further still into Father Heaven and reach for the dark/light of the Moon, who gently overshadows the mystery of the dark with her light.

- See Indigo light tendrils extend fully upwards and outwards from the top of your pranic cord, literally expanding into the vastness of the non-local, spiritual intelligence of the Cosmos.

- Notice that as these lines of force extend upwards they also seek out contact with the light of the Moon, and so make connection through your light tendrils with the Moon's surface, and gently coalesce within her body.

- Check your spine is fully aligned, and feel your feet or coccyx touching the ground, then breathe in the Light of the Moon seven times, allowing the light to mix with the indigo light of Raziel, the Angelic Companion of Anubis.
- See the White Light of the Moon permeating through the whole of your being, nourishing the cells with its energy.
- See this light reach the hundred trillion cells of your being, shining like stars and allowing the light to disperse any negativity, healing any corruption, resolving any conflict, soothing any woe – whether it be conscious or unconscious.
- Then chant the *OM* seven times, feeling the kiss of God from the sound, allowing the vibration of the Divine *OM* to resonate throughout the entirety of your SAHU.
- Then pause, and reflect.
- Observe the unique vibration moving through you, as the Moon makes profound connection with you. This will nourish you and allow a sense of divine bliss to be bestowed upon you… for now it is time to meet Anubis.
- Pause, relax and observe.
- Imagine you are standing before an extraordinarily large wooden door, with the symbol of Anubis (the Jackal-Headed God of the Dead) upon it, for this is the Palace of Great Anubis.
- See a green ray of light (the light of your soul's love) exuding out of your heart towards the door.
- This is your soul's key for the Door of Life and of Death, this is a talisman you were given many thousands of years ago – each soul has one; it's just that many have forgotten.
- As the green ray meets the door, notice how it automatically unlocks the vast doors, as your truthful, humble intention to meet Anubis, protected by Raziel (the Angel of the Mysteries) and Shamael (the Angel of Divine Guidance) emits from your heart.
- Enter into the Palace of Great Anubis, and see the vastness of the interior dimly lit by vast torches, burning in braziers attached to the walls; smell the beautiful smell of Violet Perfume hanging in the air, emitted by thousands of incense burners; hear the rapture of beautiful music wafting through the air, giving the impression of many choirs simultaneously chanting the *OM*; see fantastic

furniture distributed throughout the space, covered in rich fabrics, and feel the energy vibrating a love and wisdom that surpasses all description.

- As you move through the space, feeling as though you are levitated through it, notice that you are magnetically drawn by unseen currents towards the deep inner recesses of the space, which intuitively you know is the sanctum sanctorum of great Anubis.
- Just as you observe this, suddenly the presence of Anubis appears, and so kneel in obeisance, and feel Anubis blessing your soul by placing his hand over your whole being.
- The stream of consciousness between you is immediate, and so feel yourself in telepathic contact with Anubis, an intelligence that will reach into the inner folds of the core of you.
- You may ask anything you wish, as you are present here in good faith and pure heart, and yet you will probably want to ask Anubis about the nature of your SAHU, and how it can be amplified.
- Know that the answer will be intuitive – an oracular teaching that will arise in your dreams or meditations… whichever divine conduit great Anubis chooses. Know that this God's intelligence will arise in the time of infinite knowing for you – which could be immediately, or at a later date.
- Now that you have received this knowing – imprinted on the very glory of your soul – feel that it is time for you to humbly leave this Palace Temple, to return to the door of this place, whilst the power of the experience moves through the inner folds of your consciousness.
- This happens almost spontaneously by strength of intention, knowing, trusting that you have been in other dimensions with Anubis, Raziel and Shamael, so that you feel how you are drawn into the inner folds of your consciousness allowing for the light of your being to be illuminated.
- In a trice, notice how you are once again passing through the great Doors of Anubis Palace Temple, feeling that time and space have been traversed with great ease, as you carry this unique reckoning about the SAHU energy of your soul.
- Reflect and Relax.
- Namaste

The Angels of Atlantis want to evoke the God Anubis for you, for he is the Guardian of the Dead, the Protector of the Resurrected, and it is he who significantly overshadows the twelve keys to paradise – for they are the trajectory by which the SAHU state is entered, as a gateway to eternity.

The SAHU represents the last evidence of the physical body, and the first transformation into the eternal form of the resurrected spirit. As we open thus, we see the fully luminous form of the Etheric sheath glistening with all the initiations that we've ever been through, in all our lives. This becomes possible as the Akashic library opens to us, pouring its content meaningfully into our consciousness.

ANUBIS PROTECTION

Furthermore, the God Anubis draws our souls into the Halls of the Dead at our departure from flesh. This is the beginning chamber of the *Duat* – the underworld where all the Gods and Goddesses exist. This Hall of Truth was one of the major chambers for the SAHU, and forms a touching-point between the mundane world of the flesh and that of the Underworld. It was believed by the ancient Egyptians that souls used tombs or chambers to engage in the miracle of travelling back and forth to the Duat.

A Course In Miracles says: *Miracles are everyone's right, but purification is necessary first!* It is through the truth of love that we become pure, and so the major significant route that we can take in the preparation of the SAHU is by examining what takes place in our head and our heart, and if we can fully comprehend that no injustice, shame, untruth, or any transgression, can touch the true core of who we are, we receive the greatest prize of all, we learn the essential part of our core vibration, and so prepare for true transcendence through the AKHU.

URIEL

ETERNAL COMPANION

NINE

THE AKHU

O my mother Nut, spread yourself over me, so that I may be placed among the imperishable stars and may never die.

– THE EGYPTIAN BOOK OF THE DEAD

The ancient Egyptians believed that their ancestors were the AKHU – the Shining Ones – and that the spirit of the ancestors ascended into heaven at the point of death to become the starry belly of Nut, to become the stars that twinkle in the heavens forever.

Nut was one of the oldest deities in the Egyptian pantheon, being the Goddess of the Sky, of all the heavenly bodies, and was held as a symbol for protecting the dead after they had entered the after-life. According to the ancient legends, the heavenly bodies —such as the sun and moon — would make their way across her body during daylight. Then, at dusk, she would swallow them, so that they could pass through her belly during the night, to be reborn again at dawn.

With this in mind and heart, when you venture forth at night, look up and, as you peer into the belly of Nut – the Goddess of the Sky–, you will see your forefathers and foremothers twinkling down at you. These are the AKHU – the Shining Ones – please honour them by creating an altar for your ancestors. As you do this, you will complete their lives, venerating them for their purpose in your life, thereby healing any lesions that may have been sustained, sanctifying your profound connection – so that just as the cycle of life is made sacred by the realm of the Earth, the realm of Spirit is then wholly revered.

Please say this prayer to honor your dear ones:

PRAYER FOR THE DEAR AKHU ONES

Dear Majestic Anubis and Gracious Raziel
Please honour my Mother and Father, and all my Ancestors,
See that their spirits were brave and honourable.
Oh, Mighty Anubis, as you weigh the hearts of these dear ones,

know that they were loved by many, they will be remembered by all and will be honored by me.

Oh, Profound Anubis, please welcome my dear ones, and deem them worthy of entrance, so that they may walk through your kingdom and that of Queen Nut.

May they be under your protection for the whole of eternity, being taught by the magic of Archangel Raziel.

Oh, Mighty Anubis, please watch over my life and loves as I bow before you.

Amen, Amen, Amen

Rest a moment, and reflect on the deep resonance of these feelings in your life. Sense these beings in their light, whether you felt a connection whilst they were in flesh or not. The point is that your soul chose these relationships for a purpose, and their being-ness is traced within your genetic blueprint and energy circuitry. Deduce what the purpose of the relationship was, particularly if it was disorienting, disconnected or disappointing. Ponder on this, for there is always a reason why you chose to explicitly co-create with them, embarking as you did on your implicit journey of incarnation.

HOLDING ANCESTRAL KARMA

Being caught by the karma of anger, blame, or a lack of forgiveness, is severely debilitating; as these states move us from our core vibration, they scribe love-less-ness on the richness of our hearts. Instead, we must see the people who evoked negative emotion within us as glorified in the eyes of God. God forgives wholeheartedly and therefore so can we, instead of holding on to the negativity, foolishly attempting to use our ego to justify our loathing, which never leads to peace.

When we firstly align with our AKHU, we move into the oasis of spiritual cleansing, because being spiritual means a sanctification of wholeness. Spiritual healing is a movement back to our core, whereby we claim each part of ourselves as fragments of the Divine.

There is no way that we can feel the loving embrace of spirit if we are emotionally contaminated. However, when we're cleansed, we're instantly uplifted onto a higher frequency, and the forthcoming provocative poem by Oriah the Mountain Dreamer is expressly written to determine how to do just that. It will encourage you to think beyond the superficial, to look deeper into your life, and indeed into your soul's process, to determine how you truly feel about the consequential matters of the spirit in your life.

Do not allow a stone to remain unturned, let the conviction of your desire develop your AKHU shining body through your passionate enquiry, and you will experience your chakras' and energy field expanding richly and capaciously to accommodate the fuller light emission. At the same time, you will find the Mountain Dreamer poem courageous and investigative, functioning as a testament to your soul's shimmering. It was written specifically in order to aid you with the weighing of your heart, helping you to bravely search, by scouring your subconscious, or unconscious, mind for any inappropriate holdings or emotional waste, and thereby, you will shift into the circumference of your infinite potential.

THE INVITATION

It doesn't interest me what you do for a living. I want to know what you ache for, and if you dare to dream of meeting your heart's longing.

It doesn't interest me how old you are. I want to know if you will risk looking like a fool for love, for your dream, for the adventure of being alive.

It doesn't interest me what planets are squaring your moon. I want to know if you have touched the centre of your own sorrow, if you have been opened by life's betrayals or have become shrivelled and closed from fear of further pain. I want to know if you can sit with pain – mine or your own – without moving to hide it, fade it or fix it.

I want to know if you can be with joy, mine or your own, if you can dance with wildness and let the ecstasy fill you to the tips of your fingers and toes without cautioning us to be careful, to be realistic, to remember the limitations of being human.

It doesn't interest me if the story you are telling me is true. I want to know if you can disappoint another to be true to yourself; if you can bear the accusation of betrayal and not betray your own soul; if you can be faithless and therefore trustworthy.

I want to know if you can see beauty, even when it's not pretty every day and if you can source your own life from its presence.

I want to know if you can live with failure, yours or mine, and still stand on the edge of the lake and shout to the silver of the full moon "YES!"

It doesn't interest me to know where you live or how much

money you have. I want to know if you can get up, after a night of grief and despair, weary and bruised to the bone, and do what needs to be done to feed the children.

It doesn't interest me who you know or how you came to be here. I want to know if you will stand in the centre of the fire with me and not shrink back.

It doesn't interest me where or what or with whom you have studied. I want to know what sustains you, from the inside, when all else falls away.

I want to know if you can be alone with yourself and if you truly like the company you keep in the empty moments.

[By generous and kind permission of Oriah the Mountain Dreamer who has allowed me to quote her poem from the wondrous book, *The Invitation* © 1999. Published by HarperOne, San Francisco. All rights reserved. Oriah can be found at: www.oriah.org]

AN INVESTIGATION OF THE INVITATION

To explore further these wise and beautifully crafted words will stir the deep silt of your emotional body, until fresh tears pour to shift the emotional debris, releasing the unexpressed, and healing the wasteland. These poetic thoughts catch us mid-breath – their poignancy surprises, their transparency works like crystal sound to open and elevate, and all in good time, for they expose the silted strata of the undetermined crises in our lives. These promptings will enlighten the dark impressions of your shadow, those dark places that lie limpid and cruel until, at last, your life lit by the Divine within you draws your attention to that you were unaware of.

Suddenly your pulse will change, suddenly your breath will alter to an excited rhythm, suddenly a deep sigh will arise from your belly, your heart, and action will demand something completely new.

Many of the thoughts and feelings within Oriah's poetic statement are a joyous celebration of life, and yet the following sharp and salient pointers will also emerge encouraging you to ask deeper questions of yourself. They will cleanse your emotional intelligence, they will wash you clean, they will take you to another level of much richer transparency, they will ask of you to truly determine the way you feel.

This request will take you into the gymnasium of your soul, bidden by contrast, framed by clarity, caressed by new spiritual paradigms, you will be required to muscle up to life, so that no indecision can lead you to imprecision.

My experience suggests that whilst many of us feel the degrees of our emotion, yet we are seldom clear or honest about what we're truly feeling, for we're seldom transparent about how the feeling impinges on the fabric of our souls. Our three dimensional lives must be enlivened by emotional honesty, and my life and work have led me to observe that few of us really know how to identify what our feeling experience is, in the sense of what the emotion is called. So here, determine what are you truly feeling about the promptings from The Invitation, and see if you can invigorate your heart to such a degree that new life is awakened within, which is usually preceded by an aspect of self needing to die.

Martin Luther King said: *A man who won't die for something is not alive.* Let's interweave with this emotional courage, realizing that Dr. King meant dying to the lack of mercy in our hearts, dying to the rage in the soul, dying to the judgment in our minds, and dying to the hatred in our daily moments.

The following questions and answers will open an enquiry into your feeling strata, allowing you to see how to illuminate your body further within the infinite potential of becoming an AKHU – a shining one!

THE REALITY CHECK: QUESTIONS

1. Can you easily access the archetype of the **Divine Fool** within you – the jokester who finds fun and play in all things? The Fool is that wonderful aspect of human nature that adores funny things, the trickster who longs to eke out the pleasure of humour, the playful prankster who delights in the magic of laughter. You see, laughter helps us access the inner child, whereby we often express dark emotions, bringing healing to our vision of life.

2. Can you sit with the emotional pain in yourself or another, without wanting to hide it, or fade it, or fix it? If you truly can, you know the character of 'pain', and no longer need it to highlight what needs changing in your life. If you are undisturbed by the expression of authentic feeling in others, if you can be empathetic rather than sentimental, you are well on the way to transformation.

3. Can you disappoint another by holding prime beliefs about your own life, without bearing the grimace of arrogance, or are you easily swayed by the perceptions and opinions others?

4. Can you feel the 'slings and arrows of outrageous fortune'; can

you feel the accusations and statements of betrayal from those you know, or don't know, without betraying who you fundamentally believe yourself to be?

5.   Can you be fearless in faithlessness, in order to be fully trustworthy to your essential belief about what is good, and pure, and honest within your life?

6.   Can you experience failure, perceiving its force merely as the result of a certain action, or do you wither from the fear of failure, feeling you will never achieve your life goals?

7.   Can you be alone in the belief of being **All One**, or do you seek out co-dependent relationships, to muster your own incomplete sense of self?

THE REALITY CHECK: ANSWERS

1.   Fundamentally, the archetype of the Divine Fool represents that quality of expression that enables us to speak undauntedly, right from the heart as the kingdom of the soul. This is the force that moves one to risk openness and honesty in all of life's endeavours, even when authority wishes to silence you, even when you stand fearlessly facing the contagion of other people's denial.

The Fool lives through the breath of freedom, always looking for adventure, independently honouring the call to exercise his or her creative potential, irrespective of what others may think or say. This maverick nature evokes levity in all serious matters, finding fun in those situations that are austere or pompous, living life through a flow of delight when nothing is to be taken too seriously. The Fool always sees through any falsehood or disguise, perceiving the truth beneath the veneer. If you dare to laugh, you are a lover of life, and fully engage in the happiness project!

2.   Being within emotional pain, whilst filtering it deeply into one's fibre, is a crucial aspect of healing – so long as one isn't suffused with the drama of it all, as long as one can begin to see the value of the experience. If the significance of what one processes, the true pith of what one is feeling, isn't respected, consequences occur that blunt the sharpness of our passion. I believe moving oneself too quickly through an emotional state occurs as a result of embarrassment, shame or denial, or as a result of believing that someone shouldn't weep, just in case the depth of feeling expressed is inappropriate for the social con-

text. Generally speaking, fixing or fading in this way occurs because the witness is inhibited or upset at the truth expressed.

Yet this is very different from holding onto the wounding of the story, by repeating it time and again. When this is experience, we are not seeing the lessons that can be learned from the crisis.

3.   Disappointing others when you don't believe in their opinions, simply indicates that they are no longer congruent with your essence, and so fly to fresher waters. We can only disappoint if we appoint, and so this could be an opportunity to discern whether you are co-dependent in your relationships. Co-dependency indicates an imbalance of regard for love, and co-dependent people have a tendency to behave in passive or excessively servile ways. This means one's relationships are created in order to feel complete within one-self. If this is so, you will always feel incomplete. Dependency indicates a commitment that bolsters an uncertain sense of self, a false statement of your own true identity. Conversely, finding someone to share your own sense of completion with means you are free to experience the glory of your own freedom, within the loving interconnectivity of an intimate bond.

4.   Bearing the scorching taunts of accusation and betrayal can be truly challenging. Einstein suggested that *great spirits have always encountered violent opposition from mediocre minds*. Maybe you have experienced retribution on this scale. Yet, surely the point is that when you hold a belief as sacred, if you feel this belief is a core vibration of your soul, if you vision its integral quality from a position of flexibility, no one has the power to take the belief from you. Firstly, discern, is the belief an illusion, or a reality?

5.   Is it possible for you to be faithful to your core beliefs when you break trust with another? Does it matter if you are perceived as faithless so long as you hold a soul principle by the firm muscle of trust? These are powerful moral issues that turn our emotional compass by 360 degrees. Moving through the vicissitudes that exercise us thus, strengthens our souls, and if we were to review the lives of extraordinary people like Mahatma Gandhi, Martin Luther King or Nelson Mandela, we may clearly see how they changed universal perception through their humble ideals, even whilst their faith was severely tested.

These visionaries were accused, tortured and imprisoned by

dogmatic opinion. Gandhi said: *First they ignore you, then they laugh at you, then they fight you, then you win.*

In order for us to fully engage in the shifting point of our spiritual liberation, in order for us to tender the vine of our spiritual maturity, in order for us to till the deep soil of our soul, we often unconsciously choose desperation rather than inspiration. In light of this, and in order to transform you onto a higher octave, to awaken you to a higher degree of your soul's intelligence, to elicit service from you for your brothers and sisters whilst you openly give the jewels of your spirit, you will often be called to great tests, where the might of your mettle is shaken.

This can be when the essence of your LIGHT, that aspect of your soul which is of quantum force, is brought more fully into alignment with your three dimensional nature. This really means that the very core substance of your soul's fibre is brought into question as you suffer the slings and arrows of outrageous fortune, and yet still keep moving, still keep creating.

6.   What is failure to you? Is it a mass of unconscious memories kindled by the fire of frustration and anger about not passing certain childhood tests? Is it a continuous flow of victim consciousness, where the Martyr within refuses to surrender or yield up the pain of denial or rejection? Is it that your consciousness is not congru- ent with the norm, and therefore you've felt deeply challenged by attempting to achieve tasks that were beyond your ken? Is it that your consciousness feels rejected or stamped with the branding iron of disapprobation? These are some of the myriad reasons for why we experience failure, and there are millions of behavioural consequences that accrue. Yet, put in simple terms: 'failure' is simply the result of something we haven't accomplished!

7.   Whatever your state, look upon **failure** as the result of a mistake, a 'missed take' then take again. Yet, in this new position, calculate all your risks, for if we fail to prepare, we prepare to fail. On this occa- sion, determine what you want the outcome to be, literally tease out a strategy for how you can achieve the substance you want. Then decide what you want to feel when you've acquired success. The main thing is to keep the main thing the main thing, and then we reach the summit of our aspirations. However you must feel what you want to

experience the accolade of achievement, rather than fixating on the past where you possibly felt extremely uncomfortable about loss. In the eyes of the soul, there is no loss – failure is not fatal, success is not final, it is the courage to continue that counts.

8.   Many of us are disconnected from the Source, and so we constantly feel the gripping fear of loneliness, the wrench of aloneness, the recriminating low self-esteem, the torture of loss, the wince of scarcity, the spectre of denial – all these and more haunt our backs at every turn. Conversely, if we were to reconnect with the Source through one or twice a day being engaged in a spiritual muscular practice; if we were to believe the Source to be an infinitely unfolding creative possibility full of abundance, love and joy; if we were to believe in God's wisdom, we would discover there is no fear, scarcity or loss. In such a state, we wake to the bountiful abundance of the Universe, richly teeming with the flow of loving energy.

Shakespeare says through Hamlet: *There is nothing either good or bad, but thinking makes it so.*

If we could only see that our lives on planet Earth are genetically designed as part of a cosmic experiment through which we can recreate the Divine in Human form, our reconnection with Source would become so immediate that miracles would instantly occur. Every living thing functions through interconnectivity, every life form is vibrantly alive as a consequence of the contrasts that make up duality, every living being is blueprinted with perfection, and so is the resonating energy field of the Source.

Perhaps feeling alone and separate from life occurs because we don't have congruence with a social group that most nourishes our energy. This could be for a whole host of reasons – dysfunctional behaviour within your family, the fact that you harbour emotional lesions that need resolving, or that life is a product of fear brought on by the challenging influences of your past caregivers and experiences.

The important thing is to choose what you wish to do about it, liberate your consciousness through a path of healing with a skilled counselor, and then bravely and simply spend energy on achieving more joyous experience of this heaven called Earth.

A VISION OF TRANSCENDENCE

Spiritual transcendence challenges us to detach from the emotional dramas of any given situation, to detach from taking things too personally, to detach from the anger, impatience or injustice that comes through the Ego's determination to be right, to detach from gravity, and fly with the grace of Angels. This of course doesn't mean to say that we become aloof to the pain, the anger, or the recrimination, for they are all indicators showing whether we are in flow with the Universe or not.

They fully illustrate if we are within core vibration, or not. When we release our Ego that sees emotion as a means to create chaos, we see a point to these feelings, for when we hold them as sacred, they heal us. Thence they uplift us, freeing us from the poison.

Each moment in time, we grow towards our divine perfection. Each holy instant leads us to salvation – look at the revolution that is taking place concerning healing the tyranny of the Ego. To the Ego, the idea of eternal innocence is an absurdity, because guilt is the Ego's master. Yet, as we shift beyond the trappings of the Ego, we move beyond the conviction that guilt, suffering and despair are good for us. We literally manoeuver ourselves one step at a time, one lesson at a time, one healing at a time, closer and closer to the expression of our limitless divine potential.

DEVELOPING THE AHKU

Here on Earth, once healed, the AKHU light body helps us achieve the status of illumination. This means the immortal, divine part of our soul becomes unified with the higher self of our human potential. This means that a unification of human purpose and soul fusion allows an immeasurable synthesis to take place, a force that illuminates the transfigured spirit of the individual into a flame of fire – like the veritable phoenix rising from its ashes.

In Atlantis as in Egypt, this was achieved by being at one with a significant Star or Star System, of being at one with the ancestors, and therefore with one's lineage. Being in AKHU means the soul or BA is made one with God and universal splendour, which of course exists way beyond our limited field of locality, yet is still within reach, if we choose to extend our minds towards it.

What is true is that we are beloved children of God, and nothing needs to be done by us to make that true, for that truth was established in our creation. You see, our perfection is an inherent creation of God, and what

God created cannot be undone. In this, your connection with the stars is limitless.

Yet what does this really mean? And so I'm including here the brilliance of Deepak Chopra's vision – of the stars that we are, and the stars that others can be, to help us interpret what that can feel like.

THE CELLS OF CO-CREATIVE CONSCIOUSNESS

When you were first conceived, you were just a double strand fertilized ovum. This ovum then divided fifty times. In only fifty replications, you had become a hundred trillion cells, and this is more than all the stars in the Milky Way Galaxy.

Each of these cells is estimated to perform every second about six trillion tasks, and every cell instantly knows what every other cell is doing.

How does a human body think thoughts, play a piano, kills germs, remove toxins, and make a baby all at the same time? Whilst a human body is doing all of this, it also tracks the movement of the stars and planets, because your biological rhythms are actually the symphony of the Cosmos.

*There's an inner intelligence in your body, and that inner intelligence is **Consciousness**. This supreme genius is the ultimate power, which mirrors the wisdom of the whole **Universe**.*

–*DEEPAK CHOPRA*

BEING A STAR

Becoming a Star – believing in oneself as a Star-seed – means that we connect with all the other Stars, and this leads us closer and closer to the Galactic Heart. This is how the Pharaohs of Egypt attempted to achieve a direct trajectory to their beloved zenith, to be at one with the Galactic Heart. They saw themselves shining through their light body, with a seemingly incalculable belief in the fact that there exists within each of us, especially within the anointed ones, a place which is completely free from disharmony. This place never feels emotional confusion or physical pain, this place cannot age or die, this place experiences no sense of limitation or scarcity, this place is a quantum space of limitless possibility. But you have to choose it, and this the Pharaohs did by a constant and continual meditation on the purity of existence, whilst experiencing a series of stellar initiations in the major Temples of Egypt.

These magical rituals, profound meditations and arcane practices were conducted by the High Priests of Path, whose rites enabled the anointed one to become so connected with inter-galactic energies that he or she literally experienced what it was to embody star-ness – to become a **Shining One**!

The majority of their unique Temples were built upon epicenters of great potency, created by converging ley lines that meet at astro-geographical hot spots, linking heaven and earth in a divine geometry.

PHARAOH AKHNATON AS A STAR

Now take a star-being such as the Pharaoh Akhnaton, a name that means the living spirit of Aton or God. He was a Pharaoh of the eighteenth dynasty – ruling for 17 years before dying in 1336 BC. Akhnaton's name to fame was that he abandoned the traditional Egyptian polytheistic belief system, and introduced worship that was centered on Aton alone (sometimes written as Aten).

Indeed, an early inscription likened Aton to the Star Sun we have at the core of our Universe. Pharaoh Akhnaton would use the unique energy of the Temples to connect with the different degrees of Star force, whether with the Sun itself, or all the other Stars in the Heavens. Our Sun is part of a spiraling galaxy called the Milky Way, and lies about two-thirds of the way from the centre to the edge. The Milky Way itself contains about five hundred million stars, and holds a total mass equivalent to 1.9 million Suns.

Akhnaton would have been tutored in all this, and so his chosen name proclaimed him as an AKHU, an immortal ruler and, by this vibration, he lived as a reflection of the AKHU for his people, formulating, through divine meditation and magical practices, the constant embodiment of light in human form.

ARCHANGEL URIEL AS A STAR BEING

Another shining star appears in the form of Archangel Uriel, who overshadows the AKHU as the Angel of Eternal Companionship. Uriel is similarly known as the 'Flame of God' or 'the Regent of the Sun' – titles that were gained by performing the role of both Cherubim & Seraphim. He stood at the gate of the Garden of Eden with an everlasting sword of flame. Indeed, Uriel's list of appointments and titles became so numerous, so rich with significance, that this beautiful Angel simply became known as "one of the immortal Angels that companions the undying God". One of Uriel's most outstanding commissions was to sanctify Adam at his point of death, aid this original man move into full AKHU status.

The Orb of Uriel is pink in colour and represents the union of Heaven and Earth, made manifest through the beauty of the human heart – the seat of the soul. It is the fruit of the marriage between the herald of the red ray, and the divine awakening of the white ray, so in this form the pink ray cascades forth representing unconditional love, the magic of the love that transforms the self, and moves all onto a level of spiritual maturity that conspires with the AKHU.

This is the incandescent love that is rich with 'charisma', for he who possesses this power will be faithful to the notion of a completely open heart. These are they who are warm to others, using reassurance, calmness, empathy, and inspiration, whilst touching the hearts of the collective. Abundance, freedom, compassion and delight are their catchwords – abiding love is their compass.

Archangel Uriel as the Divine Companion maintains a powerful link with the knowledge of our life's journey, and shines light onto our path, catches us if we stumble, for the beauty of this Angel's love is supreme, and therefore Uriel's particular power is to call our souls back to our bodies, when trauma or challenge has led them to leave as we forget our limitless connection with the divine.

You see, as an Angel, Lord of Powerful Action Uriel works closely with our Eighth Chakra, the centre of the Universal Heart, and therefore connects us with the notion of universal love – that within the Universe all living beings are one interconnected force. The Universal Heart Chakra is the bridge through which the soul awakens the mental body, illuminating the conviction that what is above is also below.

Uriel personifies the Divine Fire that deluges from the Universal Mind, penetrating each plane, until it reaches the physical aspect of weight, space and time. When it is present with our bodies, the fire element ignites from fusion in the Sun, and the fission in the centre of the Earth. This simultaneously awakens the fire of our AKHU, and the kundalini at the base of the spine.

So let's experience Uriel through direct kinship with Horus, and therefore begin to open the channel for experiencing the AKHU:

URIEL'S EYE OF HORUS SONIC

- Find yourself in a sacred space, whether this be within a natural landscape or your own private sanctuary.
- Create purification in this holy space by burning Frankincense or Rosemary Oil – Uriel's favourite essence – and light a candle. If you desire, play soft ambient music that elevates your mood, caresses the ether, and evokes this special intention as a sacred act.
- Prepare your body by standing or sitting with your spine aligned, feeling grounded with the Pranic Cord open – see this as a beautiful shaft of pink light moving through the whole of your spine and connecting with Mother Earth, and then with the Solar Deity.
- Create a Mudra by placing your thumb and first finger together. Feel your Heart Chakra open, exuding exquisite love-light into your energy field, and through the space around you.
- Expire all your breath through your lips on seven counts and, crossing your eyes, look upwards towards the centre of your forehead, then downwards, then relax.
- Then inspire in on seven counts, changing the Mudra so that your thumb touches your second finger, relaxing your eyes and filling your field with light. Imagine yourself within a beautiful White Orb, representing Horus's Eye.
- Breathe out again, look up towards the centre of your forehead crossing your eyes, then look downwards and relax.
- Breathe in, creating the Mudra of your third finger and thumb touching, feeling the pink of Uriel light filling the whole of you being, and pause.
- Feel love in your heart before you expire, then breathe out and as you look up crossing your eyes, then downwards, then relax.
- Create the Mudra of your fourth finger and thumb touching, and inspire the pink light, feeling love in your heart.
- Then look up towards the centre of your forehead crossing your eyes, then downwards, and relax.
- Create the Mudra with your all your fingertips touching and expire.
- Feel love in your heart as you inspire and, when full of light, look up towards your Pineal Gland crossing your eyes together, then look downwards and relax.
- Create the Mudra of placing your hands together in prayer, and expire the breath.
- Feel love in your heart before you inspire, and when fully breathed, direct the sonic chant *OM* into the centre of your skull, gently

bathing the Pineal Gland in a fusion of Divine Sona.

- On the next inspiration of the love light, visualize the whole of the Orb of White Light within which you rest, suffused with the all-seeing Pink Ray of the beneficent force of Archangel Uriel.

- Then expire and inspire gently, three more times, feeling the Angelic force moving through the whole of you.

- On the third inspiration, pause, seeing the Orb of light expanding through the whole of the space around you, and chant *OM* a further three times.

- Pause and say three times *RA MA TI MA RA* – "Everything sacred is blessed".

- The resonance of this process will be vast and so rest and record your reflections and oracular musings – processing the entire experience and the absolute joy of the encounter. You may feel in unique communion with the whole of universal order.

- Then, to conclude, close down the Pranic Cord, seal your energy field with a beautiful white Orb-like light, and rest.

- Namaste

TRULY TRANSCENDENT

This meditation will clearly open the shrine of the Pineal Gland, which is located in the centre of the human brain between the two brain hemispheres, and is secreted in a cache where the two thalamic bodies meet in rounded configuration. This locale is one of the most profound centres within the field of human knowing, for this is a portal where the eternal and the immediate are experienced as one – this is a centre of attention known as the Eye of Horus!

Horus's eye evokes in the AKHU clairvoyance, heightened vision, cosmic awareness, psychic ascension, thought transference, the all-seeing notion of dimensional travel, and in both Atlantean and Egyptian times was a fully functioning organ of great insight.

This visionary centre can peer through all dimensions, transcending the space-time continuum, and enabling human beings to see a way by which weightless travel throughout the Cosmos is achieved. Indeed, the symbol of the Eye of Horus that you see on the front cover of this book is both a literal and metaphoric representation of the sacred Pineal Gland, for both are wedded in a marriage of far-reaching proportion.

On the physical plane, the Pineal Gland is activated by light, has a retina, pines and cones, and is connected to the visual cortex of the brain.

At this level, it serves the terrestrial function of controlling the biorhythms of the body, directing hormones in coordination with the other endocrinology glands, to regulate the body's thirst, hunger, sexual desire and aging process.

On the non-physical plane, the Pineal Gland, touched by the effervescent vibrating light of the Kundalini, connects with Divine thought. This exquisite pinecone-shaped organ actually brings vibration from the higher octaves into the physical vehicle of the human body. Therefore, not only is the Pineal a receptor, it is also a transmitter which, when used with great wisdom, allows human beings to become AKHU and project their consciousness through the ALL THAT IS!

This means that you may visit distant loved ones, send light messages to other star systems, travel inter-dimensionally accessing other Star-systems, access libraries of thought that exceed terrestrial intelligence, receive powerful data about the enfolding destiny of the Galaxy or Multi-verse, heal powerful lower vibrational inaccuracies, and accelerate your ascension process far beyond present understanding into a fifth dimensional flow. This flow is a prism vibrating with the love-light of the Source, brought into existence by the anointing of the Christos, from which Horus springs.

This sacred lineage now caresses all our lives, as we live by the light of the Source, and are bathed in the new light recalibrations of the Solar Deity, our Star-Sun. This lineage of Horus is a unique gift, for your odyssey has drawn you through countless initiations just like the Pharaohs, and has brought you to qualify for a higher octave alignment, through the prophecy of Horus and Uriel as flames of God. See Horus as an emanation of the Christos, accompanying Archangel Uriel, whose function as the faithful Companion will guide your life through the development of all twelve chakras.

The Atlanteans steadfastly ritualized the connection between all the chakras. All humans will be constantly moved to the supernal conviction of the non-local reality of love – that love is all there is. This love is the exquisite consciousness of all that exists in harmony, and so evokes companionship, communion and consortium as core ingredients within the Cosmos.

With this in mind, it's hard not to take the splendour of the Cosmos personally, beholding as we do the exquisite Star vibrating at the core of our lives. Furthermore, the gift of the higher frequency light is present as it pulses and flows through the acceleration of our cellular evolution. And so the prophecy of Horus, in parallel with great Thoth's **Kybalion** – the mystical teachings of the great Master Alchemist – is fulfilled.

In this, those who are initiated by the higher frequencies will ecstatically and instantaneously become the Homo luminous, the Human Angels, the Shining Ones.

May you rest in peace as these energies travel through you…with much love.

OM

METATRON

SUPERNAL TEACHER

TEN

THE KEYS TO PARADISE

The twelve gates were like twelve pearls, for each one of the gates was lustrous with the sheen of a single beautiful pearl. The twelve keys to the gates were shaped in exquisite carnelian, for the twelve eternal hearts that they would open. The great streets of the city were of pure gold, like transparent glass, for their gift was the gift of truth and honesty entwined. So clear were they that all who trod upon them invoked the light of sacred illumination, in fit keeping of their resonance. For this was the city of Zion, made virtuous by God's decree, and peopled by the Shining Ones who lived the highest vibration.

– A VISION GIVEN BY THE ANGELS
AS A REFLECTION UPON ST. JOHN'S REVELATIONS

The passage of time through which we currently live is daunting. More demanding than many of us wish to give credence to, more challenging than anything we've experienced for a long time – because most of the major changes required are on the inside of our beings. Of course, internal change is always multi-faceted, yet the Angels of Atlantis suggest these vicissitudes arise to enable us to create brave, new ways of living our lives, with vistas of thought and feeling that are very different from those we first envisioned living.

As we make steps to alter our internal meridians, it's fair to say that we're also challenged by world events. We are provoked by a bureaucracy, where it is difficult to find human beings who aren't scripted to produce mechanistic platitudes devoid of feeling, in work contexts where there seems to be little or no human empathy. We are roused by the staggering paucity of enlightened leaders. We are challenged by an economy where prices steadfastly rise, yet wage packets, or salary disclosures, do not evolve. We're stretched by negative reports of global disaster, and the fact that two billion people live on less than two US Dollars a day, despairing in the magnitude of their quandary. We are taxed by the fact that five thousand children die each day of hunger-related causes, and that the corruption of our own personal stress levels are so high that many of us appear to be living dysfunctional existences, hence the consequent global rise of heart disease.

Yet, at the same time, we are encouraged by all of these events to evolve into a more mature consciousness, where we don't simply explain away the crises as a conceptualized state, but muster ourselves through a deeper, more embodied grace, to experientialize our journey forward. So we release the blame and accusation thrown at the world for a more seasoned view of insight and resolution.

Of course, the world is a projection of our consciousnesses, collated on a global screen, and healed or hurt by every thought and feeling we have. If we heal the darkness of our own hurt, if we cleanse the SHEW of the individual shadow, we can truly begin to heal the world. If we use the awareness that the Keys to Paradise bring, we open a path to the miraculous, and therefore miracles occur – to the extent that we find the keys determining a level of personal transformation that ultimately changes the world.

The work the Angels give us concerns becoming the change you want to see in the world, by becoming the change that will change the world. When change is about to happen, it means we've given purpose to thought, and when action begins to happen, if we focus on the main thing as the main thing – then the main thing begins to happen.

It only takes 11% of the population to change mass consciousness, so if a section of the world's culture fully embodies spirit, we will without a question of a doubt see sweeping changes. This will occur when a unique number of us comprehend that we are spirit, and that we are more than the world; then the world itself will be in supplication to our remembering.

In Egypt at the onset of 2011, the revolution started through the action of four hundred young people on Facebook. These young ones wrote out their horror and disappointment, in review of their chaotic and despotic President and Central Government. Non-violent peaceful protest then ensued, which subsequently created the fervor of OWS (Occupy Wall Street) who remonstrated with the US Government. This is how the world wakes to remembering what happens when change occurs.

THE COMPASS OF THE KEYS

During times of great change, when transformation is acute, remaining secure means we must hold dear to the eternal jewels of life – the compassion, grace, empathy, truth, trust, gratitude, forgiveness, courage, patience, and the peerless virtue of love. If we see these as our compass, we remain steady and grounded – for they do not change. If we remain in the conviction of these gems, we always vision the best way forward. If we forget these essential facets and allow ourselves to become like pieces of flotsam and jetsam, caught by the swiftness of the fast flowing current of social change, we begin to choose the worst of ways.

When I currently feel the fast flow of change around me, when my core vibration is disturbed, my sense is that this is when I'm meant to become more centered by engaging in a deeper practice. Isn't it intriguing that some of the smaller things in life, some of the most meaningless things, can easily challenge us – the irritation of dealing with another ineffective 'call centre', the laptop file that won't open, or the printer that seems to not want to work? Yet if someone contacts me to share the fact that they're shouldering a colossal challenge – the loss of a dear one or an impending crisis – I become ultra still within, reaching into that part of me that feels no pain, that cannot age or die, that experiences no limitation whatsoever, and therefore allows love and wisdom to flow.

In the former, all discontent hinders solution, no invitation of kindness resonates from my soul, and one can't think clearly about what to do next. Whereas in the latter, my soul reaches soaring heights of tranquility, where all resources lead to limitless riches of knowing, in heart centered service to others. When I'm afflicted by the challenge I become the challenge. When I'm in core vibration I see the solution as magic. Contrast is the phenomenon, salvation is the cure, and the bliss of timelessness is the only way. And when this is amplified, wow oh wow, this becomes the modus that literally saves the world.

CHANTING FOR PEACE

Therefore, one of my major maxims has been to remind myself that, when the world is in trouble, one's need must not be to join the chaos, but to enchant the peace within. Isn't it true that the only way to gain power in a world that is over-accelerated is to slow down by calming oneself, and making sure one's behaviour has stillness? The world we wish to live in is surely not a hyperextension of our excessive doing, but a world where the still roots of our soul channel deep into the earth of our being, and the Earth of our living.

What we all need is a daily elixir of connecting with the otherworldly splendour of meditation with the Angels of Atlantis, with the rich substrata of our souls, with the deep loving dimensions of the holy instant. In these moments, we surrender to Divine will, allowing life to be what it wants to be, and allowing ourselves to be what we were created to be – *ipso facto* – we meaningfully list into a love that helps to cease the frightened nature of the world, its grim countenance, and its terrorist tactics.

For when we access Divine countenance, when we contact the Angels and Paradise by using these keys and the prana that allows us to drink in the manna, we receive spiritual nourishment that sustains us directly from the Source.

Instead of fixing our minds on the fear-based paradigms of the controlling ego, we need as Robert Browning said *to recognize a man's reach must exceed his grasp, or what's heaven for?* We must take this new perspective and look into the paradise of our lives – whether this be looking into the face of a dearly loved one, reviewing the beauty of nature, engaging in a creative activity of great enhancement, or seeing again the AKHU stars of our ancestors.

Assuredly, then, we will see an even bigger star, more massive that any other, and somewhat like the Star that heralded the Messiah Jesus. From the richness of the firmament, it will beckon us to follow, for therein we will find a wondrous birth. Yet what will emerge on this occasion is not a single birth, but one that harbours a collective awakening. From somewhere deep within our genes trumpets the sound of a new kind of human being – the Homo luminous – one who stands as a Shining One, as a radiant being.

THE SHINING WAY TO ONE-NESS

Within each thought cascades a thousand waterfalls.
Within each feeling dwells millions years.
Within each breath echoes trillions of love songs.
Within each pulse evolves the infinite of creation.

Inside each wind flows the Ocean deep.
Inside each rock sits a mighty Sage.
Inside each grain of sand resides the World.
Inside each ray of light shines the Universe.

Within each raindrop lies the Sun.
Within each blade of grass breathes the Moon.
Within each particle of soil I hear an Angel sing.
Within each tree streams the Goddess whole.
Inside each cell dwells ten million stars.
Inside each star resides an Ancestor's light.
Inside each person lives a Soul's full pride.
Inside each instant God walks soundless as the night.

Ten million stars are you, yet one Soul connects them all.
A Shining One is you, made in the perfection of the Source.

THE CITY OF ZION

In the New Testament Gospel according to Matthew Chapter 5, the scripture says:

You are the light of the world.
A city that is set on a hill cannot be hid from Zion,
Neither do men light a candle,
And put it under a bushel, but on a candlestick;
That giveth light unto all that are in the house.
Let your light shine before men,
That they may see your good works,
And glorify your Father that is in heaven.

This reveals an ancient belief about a city of Shining Ones, a mystical place known as Zion, dwelling in the higher spiritual dimensions. To the Jews, this is the sacred mountain where only the pure in heart can dwell, and the Book of Hebrews 12:22-23 states Zion is the Holy City of the living God, the heavenly Jerusalem. Arrival there marks our acceptance into the company of the Angels, Ascended Beings, and the Anointed Ones who are illumined – these are they who have perfected an integrated degree of the higher frequencies.

The aim of this promise, the aim of this great perfection, is to awaken a state of enlightenment within the body of all humans, and the objective of this initiation is to integrate the force of enlightenment, to open a bridge between the physical body, and the soul of the Divine Realm. Those who have achieved this perfection are often depicted riding on a Rainbow of Light – like the figure of the resurrected Christ in Medieval art. We see them sitting or walking the rainbow light bridge of the ANTAKARANA, the supernal bridge that symbolizes the everlasting link between Heaven and Earth.

THE BODY RESPLENDENT

It is believed by some Egyptologists that the ancient Priesthood of Egypt developed a technology by which meditative spells using magic, sound and light, and an unidentified psychotropic plant drug, were used to trigger altered states, whereby they could glimpse the rainbow bridge as a means for Cosmic Travel. Similarly, there are numerous depictions in the great Temples of Egypt of an enigmatic food being presented to the Pharaohs that heightened their powers of intuition so considerably that the Pharaohs reached a transcendental Angelic state, full of luminosity – it was believed that this process was overseen and performed by Cosmic Agents.

The power of disciplined Meditation links us to a transcendental state, linking the terrestrial and ultra-terrestrial aspect of our soul's process. As the physical and subtle bodies mingle together in a dance of light, inter-dimensional travel can be possible, and this is achieved by using the Merkabah.

THE MERKABAH

Within each of us is the universe, because everything that happens on the inside of us is also happening on the outside. At the deep part of our soul there is no world outside, because the world we know is a thought-dream of our own projection, and therefore what lies inside is an empire of feeling that emerges from within the soul, transfiguring anything on the outside. The world is thought up by each of us, and what we see is literally a manifestation of our thinking, for life is not happening to you, life is responding to you.

Have you mastered its shifts and turns, or are you floundering on the banks of the Soul's might? Wherever you may be, whatever the circumstances of your situation, remember that your life force is limitless, as you are at one with the unlimited nature of the Source.

One way of spinning into our limitless potential is by watching the deep trance-like dance of the whirling Dervish, the great turning meditation of the Sufism. For the dancers align with a supernatural force whilst dancing, which moves them into a transcendental union with the Divine. This they do as we may also, by simply opening the Merkaba.

Archangel Metatron, the supernal teacher, has gifted us the cosmic dance of the Merkabah. The dance of the Merkabah is a counter-rotating field of light around our physical being, that awakens both the dense physical and the subtle light bodies through a shape that consists of two tetrahedrons, and forming a three-dimensional Star of David; one above the other, below, and converging through the Heart Chakra.

The Merkaba is a vehicle or chariot that carries your BA from one world or dimension to another. The Merkaba enables anyone who chooses to travel through different realities – in effect to return to an original higher state of consciousness, as experienced by the beings of Atlantis and ancient Egypt, and therefore to pass over the rainbow light bridge into Zion.

MER – the light field, as two counter-rotating forms spinning in the same space.

KA – the individual spirit or soul.

BA – the spirit's interpretation of the body's reality.

Within the centre of the Merkaba is a column of light known as the Pranic Cord, which functions as a conduit to open each of the twelve chakras.

Firstly, Pranayama empowers your Merkaba 'chariot', expanding and contracting your energy field as you wish, whilst the two tetrahedron spin in clockwise and counter-clockwise directions. Secondly, a heart full of unconditional love allows the Merkaba to spin sometimes fifty to sixty feet (twenty meters) in diameter, which moves through into the love light circuitry of the Cosmos.

Let's try awakening the Merkaba:

HEAVEN'S GATE RITUAL MEDITATION

THE BREATH OF TWELVE – CREATING UNIVERSAL RESONANCE

- Prepare the sacred space in which you rest by purifying its vibration, burning incense, ringing bells, drinking water, and resonating beautiful music throughout your haven – *Spem in Allium* ('Hope in any Other') is a beautiful anthem composed by Thomas Tallis in 1570 for a choir of forty-four voices (the master number of spiritual purity) which will guide and uplift your process forward.
- Prepare your body within your Merkaba by standing with your spine aligned and the Pranic Cord open, in connection with Mother Earth and Sister Venus, and with your thumb and first finger in Mudra.
- Feel your Heart Chakra open, exuding exquisite love-light into your field and beyond into the beauty of the World, the Planet and the Universe.
- Expire all the breath on seven counts, and crossing your eyes to your pineal gland, look upwards, then downwards, to the tip of the top and then bottom of your Merkaba.
- Then inspire on seven counts through the pranic cord, from the top to the bottom, relaxing your eyes and filling your field with light,

and see the feminine aspect of your Merkaba (the lower three sided Pyramid) pointing downwards, and spin it in a counter-clockwise direction.

- Create the Mudra of your second finger and thumb touching, and breathe out all the light, and crossing your eyes to your pineal gland, look upwards and then downwards.
- Feel love in your heart before you inspire, relaxing your eyes and seeing the masculine aspect of your Merkaba pointing upwards, with the light filling your field, spinning this tetrahedron in a clockwise direction.
- Create the Mudra of your third finger and thumb touching, and expire all your breath.
- Feel love in your heart before you inspire, cross your eyes to the pineal gland, look up and downwards and relax, with the feminine aspect of your Merkaba pointing downwards, and the light filling your field as you spin it.
- Create the Mudra of your fourth finger and thumb touching, and expire your breath light.
- Feel love in your heart before you inspire, cross your eyes, look upwards and downwards, seeing the masculine aspect of your Merkaba pointing up, and the light filling your body, spinning this aspect of your Chariot.
- Create the Mudra with all your fingertips touching, and expire.
- Feel love in your heart before you inspire, cross your eyes, look up and down, with the feminine aspect of your Merkaba pointing downwards, and the light filling your field as you spin the Merkaba.
- Create the Mudra of placing your hands together in prayer, and expire.
- Feel love in your heart before you inspire, cross your eyes looking up and down with the masculine aspect of your Merkaba pointing upwards, and the light filling your body as you spin the Merkaba.
- Create the Mudra of your thumb and first finger touching, and expire.
- As you inspire the love light, visualize a ball of light in your heart chakra.
- Then expire/inspire slowly six times…
- On the seventh expiration, pause, seeing the ball of light expanding through the whole of your light field, and chant *OM…* before you inspire.

See the whole of your field lit by this divine light and ask your KA permission to connect with the Christos consciousness of theuniverse.

Your Merkaba is ready as a chariot of ascension.

TEST FLIGHT

Initially, decide where you would like to travel, and what your specific intention is. The degree to which you are able to open to unconditional love determines the degree through which you may travel in your Merkabah. Always ask your Guardian Angel to travel with you wherever you may journey. And, also ask Archangel Metatron to help you realize the key factor of your journey. The key to the process is the amount of Divine love that allows your Merkabah to become a living field of light.

Record your impressions, survey your sojourn, and monitor the sensations. Discuss what happens with a mentor or dear friend, and elicit all you can from the experience:

- What did you feel within your physical form as your Merkabah spun?
- What did you perceive about the Yin or Feminine aspect of your Star?
- What did you begin to know about the Yang or Masculine aspect of your Star?
- Where did you want to travel?
- Where did you feel your soul wished to feel its Star home?
- Where did you initially arrive?
- How did this alter your physical condition?
- How did this alter your spiritual constitution?
- How did this alter the way you regard the Cosmos?
- When did you move to your second destination, if at all?
- When did you realize what qualities your Merkabah awakened within?
- When did you feel the essence of your Star in co-creation with all other Stars?

There will be many changes in your biology, indeed in your whole countenance. Rest after this journey, drink plenty of water, stay grounded, and then close the Merkaba down by the reverse sequence:

CLOSING DOWN YOUR MERKABA

- See your Merkaba spinning, and then close down the Ying aspect of its spin.
- Breathe deeply and fully as you do this.
- See the Yang aspect of your Merkaba, and then close down its rotation.
- Breathe deeply and fully as you do this.
- Relax and pause.
- See the Chakra spinning and with your breath simply blow out each one, rather like blowing out a candle. Indeed, like candles, these powerful lights reach off into infinity, particularly through the Crystalline Grid of the planet.
- Relax and pause.
- See the Pranic Cord open and breathe in your light connection with Mother Earth – Gaia, leaving the residue in your heart's secret chamber.
- See the Pranic Cord open and breathe in your light connection with Sister Venus, leaving the residue in your heart's secret chamber.
- Relax and pause.
- Place a six-pointed Amethyst Star over your Heart Chakra, both before and behind, and spin the front Star clockwise, whilst spinning the Star behind you in a counter-clockwise direction
- These Stars are ancient protections, and will seal your Heart's Secret Chamber.
- See your energy field shimmering in a beautiful white-blue light.
- Place Silver, Green and Amethyst around the shimmering white-blue light.
- Finally place a Gold sheath all around these lights. This will seal and insulate your force, providing immense protection.
- *Namaste*

ARCHANGEL METATRON

The evolution of the Merkabah has been guided by Archangel Metatron for time immemorial. This great Archangel fulfils the archetypal role of the Supernal Teacher, for Metatron as a heavenly Orb Wanderer has been known by a host of roles, including King of Angels, Prince of the Divine Presence, Chancellor of Heaven, and the Lesser Tetragrammaton (the term 'tetra-grammaton' is derived from Greek and means the four letters that refer to the Hebrew name for God, which, when translated into Latin, become the four letters YHWH or Yahweh). Thus, Metatron in this preeminent position was charged with the sustenance of mankind and, in an ancient Cabala text known as the Zohar, Metatron is seen as being equal to the size of the whole world.

Similarly, as the Angel of Charity – charity being a heavenly gift of grace – we see Metatron as a pure reflection of the Source. In the Old Testament, Metatron was known as the Prophet Enoch. Enoch and Elijah are the only men recorded in the Bible to have been summoned by God through their Merkabah directly to Heaven, in recognition of their unparalleled purity whilst on Earth. Thus they became Angels.

In another Old Testament story, Abraham is discovered sacrificing his only son Isaac, as a sign of his obedience to God when Metatron intervenes and as the very instrument of God stays Abraham's hand from killing his son, for Abraham's obedience and humility to God were magnificent.

In another story, Moses ascends Mount Sinai wishing to see the face of God, at which point he feels the pulsating light of Metatron, for it is this great Archangel alongside Sandalphon who appears as 'the very glory of nature'.

Metatron, as the white ray of purity, is comprised of and reflects all other rays, including the supernal colours of the higher octaves that exist beyond human perception. Therefore, one may evoke Metatron by concentrating on the beautiful Diamond Ray of the Metatron icon – seen at the heading of the chapter, rather as a Star. In so doing, you will be brought unprecedented spiritual growth, for Metatron is the major dial of Angelic consciousness that calibrates divine and human force on Planet Earth, as Metatron sits on the right hand side of the Divine.

Archangel Metatron champions the **Stella Gateway** Chakra within the human energy field. This chakra contains all the information of your soul's code, including the many incarnations you have lived. When vibrating fully, this trans-personal chakra existing at the upper edge of your energy field will activate your Merkabah, and your light body will awaken to truly begin your ascension as a cosmic consequence.

Here is a meditation that Metatron has given us which will bring you into powerful alignment for the further development of your Merkabah. The idea of emptying the mind of extraneous thought, and of feeling your heart throbbing with unconditional love, is crucial for the development of the Merkabah. Once we have surrendered the debris of over-analyzing, of yielding up the negativity and worry, God's voice enters into the vacuum we create, and we substitute His thought for our thought, we become one with the Divine.

VENUS VISION – RITUAL SONIC MEDITATION

To draw Venus closer into our lives is to open a vast doorway for becoming at one with God, for Venus reigns supreme in the kingdom of heaven as the Morning and Evening Star. Venus is approximately the same size as the Earth, and appears as a yellow-saffron colour in the heavens. Over thousands of years, Venus has been revered by Earth dwellers as a symbol for the immensity, intensity and intimacy of love. Therefore, Venusian beauty (Venus/Aphrodite was the Goddess of Love) over-shone many of the Atlantean and Egyptian rituals.

- Make sure you consecrate the space, whether this be your indoor sanctuary, or an arbour in nature. Burn incense and a candle, play bells and singing bowls to revere and purify the space, open yourself within the space to a happening of rare degree.
- Choose a partner, preferably in a **male/female** balance – and if this is not possible, imagine someone of the opposite sex whom you know as pure, standing in a fully present way before you.
- Stand opposite one another with left palm upwards and right palm downwards, the palms may touch.
- Breathe deeply together, seven times, taking your time to synchronize the rhythm of your breath… seeing and circulating the breath through your right hand and then into the left hand of your partner.
- Do this seven times with your eyes closed and then pause.
- Feel each other's Merkabah open and rotating, and use the process we opened in the previous Heaven's Gate Ritual Meditation.
- Synchronize each Merkabah together by spinning the masculine aspect clockwise, and rotating the feminine aspect counter-clockwise– above and below.
- Pause and **feel the force** – perceive the Cosmic Mind of the Universe flowing through you.
- Then intend each of your **Heart Chakras** to connect through the flow of sacred Prana – use a cord of green light as a connector.
- Continue to breathe together twelve times, seeing how each other's energy field becomes bigger and bigger and bigger, stimulated by the heart flow energy.
- Then say together: *RA MA TI MA RA* (Everything Sacred is Blessed.)
- *TI RA RA MA* (Everything Blessed is Sacred).
- *RA MA TI MA RA.*

- Pause – feel the sonic glyph stir in the space between you.
- Chant *OM* – seven times on a powerful breath.
- Pause.
- Feel the **Love** of the Divine Mother and the Holy Venus flowing through you.
- Imagine a sphere of light in your heart the colour of Yellow/Saffron.
- Name it as your **Venus Vision**.
- Breathe life force into this image three times, and see the Orb become as big as your Merkaba – share the Orb with your partner
- This is **Venus** and so, as you honour her force, listen to her teachings about love.
- Pause and reflect.
- Then together allow the process to diminish – firstly seeing the sphere of Venus diminish; secondly disconnecting from your partner; thirdly stepping back and slowly opening your eyes; fourthly closing down the rotating nature of your Merkabah, then breathe deeply and be still, and at peace.

THE DIVINE PLANETARY GRID

God knows our uneven surfaces and our crooked ways. God knows the wounds in our hearts and bodies. God knows the broken aspects of our soul and incarnation. Indeed He knows all things that need repairing. The Cosmos is completely self-correcting, and so are we, being made in His image. Therefore, He is also deeply desirous of healing us too, to calm and orientate those parts of us that we have miss-created. Yet God can only heal us if we are willing to give up the pain. If we are truly willing to relinquish, surrender and atone all the 'stuff', we will be healed. However, God can't take away what we aren't prepared to release into his favour, because we are bound by free will.

God alone cannot remove these blemishes, for it is we in conjunction with 'His' force that responds to the Divine calling of utter transformation. It is we that must name the pain, surrender the lesion, yield to the fact that 'miss-created will' brought the challenge, and then ask the Holy One to remove it forthwith. It is in this moment that we experience the miracle of true transformation, when we are plugged back into the Crystalline Grid of the planet's purity, and we are cured by the Sacred Ones. It is they who spread the love-light through our life stream, through our whole psychic force.

Our errors and mistakes do not change our eternal presence – God knows this because He created us. What happens in the healing is that we are reminded of who we truly are, rather than what we have become. We are recast once we have cast out the demons. Once we atone, once we pray on bended knee, once we truly respect this calling, His spirit enters us at a deep level, deeper than any three-dimensional force, penetrating the marrow of our disassociation from Divine principle – then are we fully changed on the deep causal level of our consciousness.

The collective healings that have taken place whilst intersecting the significant dates of 11.11.11 – 12.12.12 – 21.12.12 have been enormous. Indeed the twenty-five years since the Harmonic Convergence of August 1987, right through to the Precession of the Equinoxes in late 2012, have moved us into a precise alignment with the Crystalline Grid of the Planet, and so with the Galactic Heart.

This was truly needed, as our planet's Crystalline Grid had been severely misaligned by the catastrophic explosions that took place during the end times of Atlantis, the impact of which was then compounded by the atomic explosions at Nagasaki and Hiroshima in 1945. The consequent devastation of the planet's natural resources was not just experienced on Earth, but the vibration of these atrocities spread throughout the Cosmos.

Mother Earth is loved throughout the Galaxy, and by life forms that aren't humanoid. Mother Earth as a unique bio-culture is considered extraordinary by the intelligent species that exist beyond this terra firma. Mother Earth exists as a consort of energies through which a unique Cosmic Experiment is conducted, that being 'the only planet of choice'. All exists in duality on planet Earth, providing contrasting choices – until, that is, we rearrange our focus to become aware of the fact that **all the knowledge in the world is not equal to love** – for love is all there is.

LIVING IN THE LIGHT

If we see ourselves as beings of unlimited potential, we begin to co-creatively bring about change. Yet every moment we deviate from the path we consider to be the highest choice – bringing about pain for self or others – we deviate from love. Being conscious of the Crystalline Grid is to be conscious of God at the deepest level and, at this place of divine alchemy, transformations occur because the Divine Curriculum is fully open to us. It is from this light source that we may download waves of grace that completely alter our destiny.

Meditating and feeling ourselves sourced from the grid means we acquire the ability:

- To heal oneself.
- To send love and healing to all beings.
- To instantly connect with other beings, animal, vegetable and mineral.
- To assist with personal and planetary transformation.
- To activate planetary codings that continue to promote health for all.
- To access the universal language of light.
- To develop and transmit telepathic communication.
- To link with the world in unity consciousness.
- To evolve those skills that note the expansion of consciousness.
- To communicate more easily with other dimensional light intelligences.
- To use entry and exit points for inter-dimensional travel.
- To embody a more complete sense of just knowing.

METATRON TEACHES THE KEYS

Metatron knows that it can be difficult to give birth to your spiritual potential. It may be simple to face the truth that sits between love and hate, but it isn't easy to live it. What makes it more successful, more fluid, is when we rest in the arms of God, and when we languish in the infinite intelligence of the Universe.

This occurs as we give up the struggle by surrendering to joy, releasing all the trying to be right, detaching from the opinions and prizes of the world, and seeing life as inherently abundant, for when we live this life, the end result is the love of our lives. We do not need to learn love, which is already within the quanta of our souls, but we sure need to unlearn the fear that we are unconsciously programmed by, and which stops us from feeling love.

Similarly, if we can remain open to miracles, if we can flex our senses by the knowledge that there are Angels, we forge ahead into a new realm of being, reaching unimaginable heights. These are the realms where love has healed the fear that sabotaged our path in the past.

Some of the ways of the world right now are very dark, but what the world needs now is love sweet love, and when we live in the light, loving the light, the power it bestows ultimately makes us into Masters.

METATRON MASTER THE KEYS

KHAT – This is your connection with the great light, and is primarily found within your physicality. Therefore, if we see our bodies as a lens through which we filter the light of our soul and the soul of the Cosmos, we begin to function freely as space beings on Planet Earth. A healthy Earth is a healthy body, and so we more easily discover what on earth we are on Earth to unearth about our Soul's destiny. Feeling the fullness of our KHAT means we begin to hold greater light and, through healthy conduct, we become transparent vehicles of profound intensity.

Your connection with the light is created by the inter-relationship between your light body, functioning through each Chakra, and the hologram of the Universe. Here we see the Angelic Guardians for each Chakra, and the physical element they connect us with.

METATRON	12th Chakra of the Stellar Gateway which bids – I AM GALAXY
SHAMAEL	11th Chakra of the Soul Star which loves – I AM SOUL
ZADKIEL	10th Chakra of the Cosmic Heart which selects – I AM GRACE
SANDALPHON	9th Chakra of the Earth Star which beckons – I AM YIELD
URIEL	8th Chakra of the Universal Heart who intuits – I AM CONNECTION
MICHAEL	7th Chakra of the Crown who bestows – I AM KNOWLEDGE
RAZIEL	6th Chakra of the Third Eye who sees – I AM SEEING
GABRIEL	5th Chakra of the Throat which utters – I AM SPEECH
RAPHAEL	4th Chakra of the Heart which lives – I AM LOVE
JOPHIEL	3rd Chakra of the Solar Plexus which feels – I AM FEELING
ZAPHKIEL	2nd Chakra of the Sacral which adores – I DO

HANAEL 1st Chakra of the Base which communicates –
I AM THAT I AM

KA – This is the energetic connection with your soul as a holograph. Within your KA is the blueprint resonance of your life patterns and ancestry – all the substance of what is important for you in the life of your soul or BA, and how you connect with the BA of Gaia. Indeed your KA is the holographic double of your KHAT, and most past life memories dwell within your KA, as a stage of connecting you with your multi-dimensional self.

Full opening within your KA allows you to tune into the love-light circuitry of the Cosmos which, in turn, increases your ability to make manifest the glory of your soul on Earth.

SHEW – This is the aspect of your being which holds Shadow, which integrates your subconscious with the collective unconscious, and therefore allows a way of seeing the world that is yours.

It is within the SHEW that we store all trace elements that do not allow us to live the full frequency of our soul, those fragments that we have given away to trauma, and so it is our quest to restore these aspects of our soul and therefore to live the full effect of our soul's light. Sometimes the journey of reclamation can be arduous, both in its mystical and mundane aspects yet, if we are prepared to take that path, we can then allow the fullness of our souls to shine in human flesh as they were intended to do**.**

REN – This force lives through your vibrational qualities of sound, colour and light, and these qualities interplay with form and feeling through geometry, music, art and your force of wellbeing. Journeying into REN provides us with the greatest access point of transcendental states such as being in *Theta Thought* and *Samadhi*.

Multi-dimensional force lies within REN, allowing us to see the true essence of things beyond the surface state, and into the deeper values that signify the Sacred.

AB – The human heart of the AB is the portal to the conviction of the soul, and therefore the AB balances the substance of purity, truth, honour and love – for the heart is the seat of the soul, as the Angels have repeated many times.

Once the heart is healed, and we begin to make each decision – each choice – from the heart, life begins to shimmer with an incandescent splendour, and our health immediately improves. This allows a profound empathy to grow for ourselves, as well as for others. The latter proves a key to the immense and intense way that we can tune into generosity, compassion and kindness, to all living beings – animal, vegetable and mineral.

BA – This is that aspect of our soul's connection with the Collective or Universal Soul. It is the filter for Divine light, drawing it constantly into out beings, nourishing our whole life with exquisite Pranayama – the Elixir of the Soul.

The BA allows us to develop visionary faith, so that we see through each aspect of our lives, and the people who people our lives. Inevitably, this allows us to embody or integrate our souls into our daily lives in a highly specific way, and life is never the same again, for we live as Spiritual Initiates changing all aspects of our living, and our thinking to accommodate our souls.

SEKHEM – The fire of SEKHEM can be used to purify any aspect of the shadow, for SEKHEM is the power of life force burning through our lives, producing the vital fuel of our willpower – the force that enlivens our endeavour, allowing us to reach new emotional heights, and new creative aspirations. SEKHEM is a major current to the Source, allowing our Soul to create vast transformation, opening the gates to paradise.

The counter-opposition to this immense force is the turgid nature of the shadow when fear, self-denial, hatred and anger, block the way of our personal power.

However, when SEKHEM is implicit, we use will to create the magic of our successes.

SAHU – To merge with SAHU is to merge with the Divine, allowing the very breath of God to stream through one's body, and then one's body configures the light, allowing the crystals in the body to shine the light of the Source – so we become like liquid Crystal, thence we are Crystalline.

SAHU is the transfiguration of Self into Spirit, and so God speaks directly through you to your Higher Self, and the earth-bound, temporal and temporary self merge with the Divine Rays of the infinite.

In a sense, within SAHU, we take on God's form, and so become holographic beings.

AKHU – Through AKHU, we merge with the co-creative aspect of God, we transcend into the consciousness of the Great One, and we ascend into the nature of the eternal. Incorporating this state of refined bliss in human form is why we are on planet Earth, and the more we heal the shadow, the more we move into the bliss of this possibility.

Holding the light of the Holy Ones and God can be quite an experience. Sipping the nectar of the Divine can be too much to hold, unless we are grounded and fully aligned with Source. Regular Sonic Meditation and Silent Yoga will achieve this for us.

In AKHU, the visionary state becomes a probability and not just a possibility and so we see:

To see a World in a Grain of Sand
And a Heaven in a Wild Flower,
Hold Infinity in the palm of your hand
And Eternity in an hour.

– WILLIAM BLAKE

With this capability we transcend and become a Shining One that communicates eternal peace and everlasting love with such infinite ease, that life is never the same again. Namaste

ZAPHKIEL

SACRED LOVER

ASCENSION

Life is not happening to you, Life is responding to you. The question is, what do you wish to create as an expression of your Spirit, and of your Soul? Then, when you have created this joy of your effulgence, what gift do you pledge to eternity?

– THE ANGELS OF ATLANTIS

Archangel Zaphkiel is the guardian splendour of Sacred Love, and as such also lives the role of the Angel of Compassion. Compassion arises in our midst as a gift of God's Grace, and is one of the highest vibrational influences that we humans can live. Compassion shines forth from Zaphkiel's orange carnelian ray, as a rich seam of love, in empathetic concern for the welfare of all living beings – animal, vegetable and mineral – people, plants and planet. This is the love that bubbles forth from the spring of the eternal.

Thus, Zaphkiel's glory shines forth as a beacon to remind us that we are loved, and that our purpose is to love. If we fill our beings with the force of this infinite love, our creativity becomes boundless, because from this being-ness arises infinite possibilities. Being thus means we have the ability to think in ways that make the electrical and magnetic occur and, with Zaphkiel's guidance, we begin to think in ways that attract and reflect as much love as we can hold – indeed the whole love of the world. This quality of being is 'enlightened' – it is the force that determines the best choice available to us in each holy instant.

Zaphkiel's powerful love is often seen in mystical texts such as Cabbala, where the power of this Archangel appears as a solitary presence moving through the vale of tears, where the weary, sad and forlorn ones meet. This is a quality of spiritual experience we know as the fourth dimension – a non-locality that holds souls who are still caught in the membrane of their astral body, without flesh.

These are they who do not know they have transited from life into death. These are the spirits who, as a consequence of a traumatic demise – from drug addiction, fatal accident, or ravaging murder – do not know they have passed on. It is in this dimension that Zaphkiel paces, which is just before the Gates of Paradise, offering mercy, compassion and exquisite love.

STANDING AT THE GATES OF PARADISE

Being within the capacity and scope of infinite love is our divine inheritance and so, if we ever feel at odds with the world, in the depths of aloneness, or the desolation of tears, Zaphkiel will always appear when we make the call through prayer. The light of Zaphkiel is the answer to every loving prayer, just as the very substance of enlightenment is the answer to every challenge.

Where enlightenment dwells, God dwells, shining light into every problem, and so it is solved. In any situation where conflict lives, if we can only call upon Zaphkiel as God's emissary, realizing that God dwells within each of us, there is nothing that exists which God does not have the ultimate power to transform. Saying a prayer to Zaphkiel brings this splendour forth:

> *Dear Archangel Zaphkiel,*
> *Please grant us, in this divine moment, your deep and unending passion, allowing your sacred love to inflame our ardor to the heights of a new way of loving. At the same time, please allow us to feel your gentle caress, so that we may pledge ourselves to heal through love.*
> *Please see us as those who seek compassion, so that we may surrender to the greatness of your sacred love.*
> *Please allow us the possibility of rising through grace to a richer sunset and sunrise, so that we may marvel in the glory of the Source, feeling ourselves touched by the ecstasy of your divine nature.*
> *Please bring to all of our creative outpourings a fire that provides an opportunity to reach a fruition of joy that transfixes our souls with love.*
> *And so it is.*
> *Amen*

The wonder of Zaphkiel reminds us of the love that shines from deep within the Source, that in moments of terrible isolation can be forgotten. Therefore, this Angel of Sacred Love encourages us to find the true romance of life, surrendering to the ecstasy of passion, allowing ourselves to pulsate with the joy of the dance with bliss, and in devotion to the Divine. These ideals of love have a unique shimmer within the octaves of divine emission, for they tumble from the centre of the love that exists at the core of the Galaxy.

Seeing yourself as a loving notion in the mind of God allows no vicissitude, no circumstance, to lure you from the experience of feeling the immense love. See Zaphkiel as a living notion of God's thought, showering you with love – not because of what you have achieved, but simply because of whom you are.

See the realm of your creativity, your locality, the world, the universe, the galaxy as being your personal love gift, directly arising as a token of the love God has for you. See that God is all love, and so receive His love openly, and through your whole being. Then give others an expression of this infinite intelligence.

By aligning yourself with thoughts and feelings such as these; by tuning yourself with the infinite love of God via Zaphkiel; by experiencing the nature of what this behaviour allows, you will inevitably gain dominion over the demons of the lower depths – the thought-forms that appear as tyrannical controls, stopping you from being who you truly are in your Soul.

It is with this level of iridescence that Zaphkiel watches at the Gates to Paradise, watches with such keen certainty, watches with the knowledge that the 'stir' of unconditional love is quivering in your flesh, and pulsing from your heart. Being moved thus means we truly see the ultimate possibility of Ascension. This is a vision in mind whereby we feel the breath of the next evolutionary measure for human kind, for ourselves, which exists at any stage of our spiritual sojourn.

Yet this is the time for something unique – this is a time of reckoning – this is a time for us all to open the portals of ancient wisdom, concerning the life of our planet and her people. This is a time to vision ourselves effortlessly climbing ladders to God, and in consequence fulfilling a quality of service that resonates of a higher purpose, the purpose of guiding our planet and her people through Ascension.

FLESH EMBODYING SPIRIT

Drenched in the vibration of the ancient cosmic ray of compassion, Zaphkiel now exists through the silver frequency of the Divine Feminine, arising from the very centre of the Cosmic Heart. Zaphkiel's force is transported by the phosphorescence of the silver ray, resonating straight through the electrical frequency of the soul, suffused by the very breath of God.

This is the force of the great soul that was once reluctant before entering the body of clay millennia ago. This is the soul that was enchanted by the ecstasy of the Seraphic music, and which proclaimed that there is only one choice: to be embodied in human form!

There exists an ancient story from the East that tells how God in his/her infinite wisdom made a statue of clay, an image in similar likeness to the

Infinite One. Then, God asked the Soul of the Galaxy to enter the body of clay, but the Soul refused, for to be captured thus meant all freedom would be lost. Therefore, God asked the Angels to sing Seraphic music, and the Soul became so enchanted by this magic, was so moved, that it agreed to enter the statue of clay – so began Adam Cadman – so began human life on Planet Earth: embodied in a vessel of flesh.

Zaphkiel unerringly inspires us to acts of great love, which in turn encourage us to feats of even greater personal compassion and divine romance. The nature of this love folds into our physical world through varying octaves and degrees of the Cosmos, and so cascades into our physical bodies. Then it is paramount that we be willing to be sweetly lifted by this supernal love, for upliftment brings incandescence into our carbon beings, a force that literally slips into the space-time continuum we live, illuminating our path with sublime ecstasy.

In Atlantis and ancient Egypt, Zaphkiel nurtured all aspects of life through the loving creativity of the Universe, and so Zaphkiel similarly gives us glimpses of other realities, whilst blessings of the Divine are bestowed on all. These truths imparted such sublime wisdom that spiritual growth was immediately accelerated, for Zaphkiel was the gatekeeper to the depth of conviction lying within each truth-seeker, which is the essence of divine love.

It is so for us today, and so it will be for us tomorrow, as we find the keys to paradise, allowing us a special qualification for entry into the place of sublime ecstasy known as Heaven. All we need do is to surrender our individual will to divine will, and there is no better way than through meditation. Sacred Sonic Meditation allows us to listen fully to God, and so to be within the presence of the Divine.

HOVERING AT THE GATES OF PARADISE

- Make sure you have **Silence, Solitude and Stillness**.
- Move to your Sacred Space and switch on voicemail, so that you won't be disturbed. Light a candle and burn incense to cleanse the atmosphere. Play sacred sound to similarly prepare the space and lift all to a higher vibration for your remarkable encounter with the Gate of Paradise.
- Find a chair or cushion to sit upon, feeling your spine comfortably aligned, and your body weight balanced.
- Place your hands separately on your lap or knees, and place your fingers into a Mudra, such as placing your forefinger and thumb

together. This will unite powerful energies within your physique and thence within the whole energy field.

- On this occasion, if you will, bring each of your fingertips together, creating a sacred star, to register your unique intention to receive wisdom from the depths of Paradise.
- Imagine the Pranic Cord moving through your spine generating from your heart, and see a silver laser beam of light shining through your spine.
- See the Pranic cord moving down to the base of your spine, and through the various levels beneath you – the earth, clay, stone, until you reach bedrock.
- Once there, anchor the cord of light into Mother Earth, and notice how you feel completely held by her, the force of unconditional love compassionately supporting your gravity. Ask her for a gift, a blessing, or a token and, when ready to receive, siphon that force up through the varying levels up into your body.
- Complete this by drawing the secret messages from Divine Mother Gaia up through the cord, and placing these jewels of experience into your heart's secret chamber.
- Then continue allowing the silver cord to move through the top of your spine and off into Father Heaven.
- See the cord of light move to your favourite star; if you don't know which this is, choose one, this could be a planetary home. Venus is the brightest star in the night's sky and one that benignly overshadows the work of the Temple of Sound Healing, for Venus is the Planet of Love.
- Then feel the breath from the Source as a silver force moving down through the Pranic Cord and into the whole of your being.
- Pause…then breathe all the breath out of your body.
- Wait a moment before you breathe in again and, when you breathe in, see the breath as light or colour moving through your body, like an elevator moving down through your spine.
- Breathe wide and deep with the power of the Chi, and breathe out by singing the *AH*, the Heart Chakra vowel.
- Chanting the *AH* three times will bring all of your energies into the coherence of your heart centre, which in turn will open the palace of your Soul, for the heart is the seat of the Soul.
- Visualize an Eight-Pointed Violet Star shielding the front of your Heart Chakra, about seven inches (15 centimers) in height and width.

- Breathe in, and as you sound out on the *OM,* spin the Star in a counter-clockwise direction three times. The Star is an ancient protection for your Heart Chakra, and will stimulate pranayama throughout the whole of your energy field. This in turn, with the most accurate intention of offering your individual will into Divine will, will encourage an expansion in your aura to occur.
- Feel love in your heart and allow the brilliance of your 'SHINING ONE' essence to illuminate the space around you.
- Spin the Star three times chanting *OM* and feel love for the Divine in your heart resonating a deliciously sweet resonance. The Star is an extremely ancient powerful talisman that will open your heart, as a key to the Gates of Paradise.
- Observe the heightened sensations within your body.
- Remember the intuitions you receive.
- Record the feelings of your Heart opening your Gate to Paradise.
- Sound *OM* three times to seal your field, and then rest.
- Feel the Divine Beings linking themselves around you, especially tuned to the pitch of this moment, for they know how you have worked to release your personal and ancestral karma.
- The Angels of Atlantis want you to feel their support as you enter through the Gates of Paradise, and so be aware of the talisman Star they inspired resonating through your heart Chakra.
- Close your eyes, breathe deeply, and see before you the Gates of Paradise, pictured as a vast green portal – green is chosen as the colour depicted in many ancient texts concerning the seat of the Divine
- Allow the splendour of the energy to move deeply within your heart, and therefore deeply within your soul.
- Write down the impressions received in your journal, and draw them deeply into a silent meditation, knowing that the divine *OM* permeates deeply throughout your cells.
- Before you will be an extraordinary experience of upliftment as you release the power of your own Ego into the Will of God. When this we do, we refine and transform into the Divine, which means that grace and joy lift us up, our being soars, and we feel the support of the brilliance of Zaphkiel's orange-carnelian plasmic power taking us into union with the Divine – a state that is sometimes known as Samadhi or Nirvana – and one that feels like a bliss-filled love.
- When you feel you have reached a point of completion with this process, draw in the silver pranic light from Sister Venus and from

Mother Earth.
- See your whole field shimmering in the white light of your etheric sheath, expanded, vast, in tune with the mind of God – hearing the very thoughts of the Divine.
- Place a green and then violet light over the white sheath – these colours are the vibrational frequencies of the Angels Temple, and will allow you to feel fully contained within the vastness of God's soul.
- Finally, sheath your whole field in Golden Light – this is a powerful Archangelic protection, and will help you to surrender your will to the perfection of the 'All That Is.'

LIVING IN THE GRACE OF PARADISE

The heart of man is the paradise of God, and living where the principles of grace take you means that you will receive powerful intuitions and quickened teachings directly from the Source. There may be interpretations about your past lives, your present métier, and possibly even inklings of your future lives.

Whatever it may be, wherever you may be, and so ever, the teaching you are provided and each observation will be specifically tuned to the ascended nature of your soul's evolution, enabling you to see a way towards becoming a Master or Mistress of your living spirituality. This means that your light-body will express what it is through the many manifestations of your being, and so transform itself through any **space time** portal you wish to travel to or through.

The illumination and refraction of the twelve following qualities will percolate through your life, with your own specific intention enlivening all of the details. Needless to say, the power of the light moving through the life of this planet is vast, and so these are only some of the qualities that the Angels wish me to communicate at this time. These are the salient points that Zaphkiel, and the other Angels of Atlantis, wish to bring through right now into your life.

The Divine qualities will be:
- Conscious creation through disciplined thought.
- Unconditional love shining throughout your days and your nights.
- An honouring of the physical temple your Soul has chosen.
- Grace & Compassion pulsing in each action.
- Joy & Bliss permeating the whole of your countenance.

- Gratitude filling each holy instant.
- Forgiveness percolating through each thought, word and deed.
- Non-judgmentalism shining through each breath as a cycle of knowing.
- Allegiance to Mother Earth Gaia as a totem of your life.
- Living in one-ness with the Divine Cosmic Father enlivening your days.
- Activating your **light-body** through loving thoughts, as your only wish.

PRAYER OF AFFIRMATION

I am Soul
I am Divine Light
I am Love
I am Divine Will
I am Grace
I am in touch with Core Vibration
I am the One and Only Light of the Sages
I am with the Source
I am Peace of Mind
I am the Divine Plan on Earth
I am Peaceful Joy
I AM THAT I AM
I am Living Divine Light in Human Form

- Drawing the light of the Source into our bodies is why we are here.
- Living the light of the Source in flesh is why we chose Planet Earth.
- Realizing that we are never alone is why we are here.
- Always reaching for the highest point of our creative evolution is why we are here.
- Disseminating **Love** is why we are here.
- Singing the pure song of the ancient ones is why we are here.
- Venerating Mother Earth Gaia is why we are here.
- Remembering Father Heaven above is why we are here.
- Communicating with other Star-Being Brethren is why we are here.
- Being at one with the abundance of nature is why we are here.
- Living the wonder of life through breath is why we are here.
- Expiating personal, family and planetary Karma is why we are here.

AND SO IT IS FROM THE ANGELS

The Universe, as God's creation always knows what you want and need. The Universe is inherently programmed to bring forth abundance for eternity. This means that the Universe knows exactly how to transform all energy into the creative force that is necessary to sustain qualitative evolution and positive growth on this planet, and of course within this part of the Galaxy.

Your venerable task must simply be to purify your heart, and then your force will become a veritable dynamo for receiving and giving abundance, wealth and miracles. For you are a thought in the mind of God, you are one of God's ideas moving through a process of unfolding, and this thought that is you is constantly fed by the Cosmos. This thought that is you has a constantly evolving role within the role of the Universe and, as God is a love that is infinite, you share in that love, for you are that love. Please know this is the truth of who you are.

You are a wave in the unending evolution of the Cosmos, in the ever-evolving Mind of God you are a miracle, and as God is an eternal fountain of miraculous possibilities, the spirit of God has great things in store for you. God is asking you to become the idea that God had of you – for you are God's gift to the world – and, with this in mind, you will begin to release, through creative expression, the unlimited potential that is within you – the ability to be true, to express goodness, and to emanate beauty.

This is not spiritual arrogance, this is opening you to the revelation of your spiritual magnificence, this is the recognition of the spirit within you, which honours your value, just as it loves the infinite value in all of us beings. This is the love of God emanating from you, asking you to dedicate your life and work to the purpose of healing the world.

This is our common aim, as a spiritualized function of the Universe, as a wave of boundless loving abundance flowing in the playfulness of the Universe, and this is the only way that we can be with joy, by fulfilling this spiritual task as we flow with the Universe, which is the Supreme Mind.

Namaste,
– The Angels of Atlantis.

FINDHORN PRESS

Life-Changing Books

For a complete catalogue,
please contact:

Findhorn Press Ltd
117-121 High Street,
Forres IV36 1AB,
Scotland, UK

t +44 (0)1309 690582
f +44 (0)131 777 2711
e info@findhornpress.com

or consult our catalogue online
(with secure order facility) on
www.findhornpress.com

For information on the Findhorn Foundation:
www.findhorn.org